Praise for *Pande.*

If I had to select just three words to
Inc.," I would pick wisdom, creativi~~y~~, ...~~w~~ usefulness.
Alfredo Romero Vega, Director,
PROFIT Consultoría e Inversiones S.A.C.

Patrick Schwerdtfeger has an uncanny ability to consistently see ahead of the curve and does so once again in his newest book, "Pandemic Inc." Similar to his book "Anarchy, Inc.," he takes the current state of affairs and looks beyond them into the future. While not necessarily creating a defined roadmap for any one industry, he outlines a framework to ask the right questions, identify opportunities, and plan ahead. I would highly recommend it to owners and managers of businesses large and small.
Mackenzie Singleton, Founder, Barton Branding

"Pandemic Inc." took me on a journey into a possible future based on eight accelerating trends of COVID-19. Schwerdtfeger lays out how these eight trends could impact businesses and societies around the globe. His SALVAGED acronym makes it easy to understand each trend individually as well as collectively. I thoroughly enjoyed reading "Pandemic Inc." and now feel better prepared to capitalize on many of these trends in my own business.
Richard Franzi, Renaissance Executive Forums,
Orange County

Patrick Schwerdtfeger has written an insightful analysis of the current coronavirus pandemic and its possible outcomes. "Pandemic, Inc." is essentially a message of hope. Patrick writes, "If you can look beyond the hardship and struggle, this is a very exciting time! Opportunities are around every corner, and people are desperate for solutions. You will only benefit from this situation if you see it as an opportunity." The world is entering a period of historic disruptive change, but from chaos will come great growth.

Eric Wentworth, Author of "A Plan for Life"
(2014, Charles Stephen Publishing)

In "Pandemic, Inc.," Patrick Schwerdtfeger shares insights into several business trends that are accelerating as a result of the coronavirus pandemic. He synthesizes the complexities of disruptive innovation into easy-to-consume, actionable ideas that add immediate value in thinking, planning, and acting strategically. Schwerdtfeger's Strategic Questions section at the end of each chapter will inspire organizations of all sizes and types to come up with ways to turn today's change into tomorrow's growth opportunities. Leaders committed to their own development as well as the success of their organizations 'can't not' read this important book.

Cathleen Hoffman, MBA, SHRM-SCP, SPHR,
Arkansas Human Resource Professional

YOU NEED THIS BOOK! There are many authors who identify problems, but "Pandemic, Inc." offers tactical guidance to profit from them. Schwerdtfeger has a unique way of taking complex financial and technological issues and making them clear and understandable. In this book, he provides the reader with a clear guide to the new world that we are rapidly entering. You'll be blown-away by the implications and certainly better prepared by reading "Pandemic, Inc."

Louie B. Free, BrainFood from the Heartland, The
Louie B. Free Radio Show

PANDEMIC, INC.

BY PATRICK SCHWERDTFEGER

Pandemic, Inc.
8 Trends Driving Business Growth and
Success in the New Economy
by Patrick Schwerdtfeger

1. BUS070020 2. BUS070140 3. BUS07003
Paperback ISBN: 978-1-949642-40-7
Hardcover ISBN: 978-1-949642-41-4
Ebook ISBN: 978-1-949642-42-1

Cover design by Lewis Agrell

Printed in the United States of America

Authority Publishing
11230 Gold Express Dr. #310-413
Gold River, CA 95670
800-877-1097
www.AuthorityPublishing.com

PANDEMIC, INC.

8 TRENDS DRIVING
BUSINESS GROWTH AND SUCCESS
IN THE NEW ECONOMY

BY PATRICK SCHWERDTFEGER

*This book is dedicated to
all small business owners.*

ACKNOWLEDGEMENTS

Many people had an impact on this book. First and foremost, Richard Franzi, you recommended me to Kim Hibler, John Affleck, and Julio Noriega, all from Renaissance Executive Forums, to do a webinar about the pandemic and its effects on businesses. That opportunity led directly to the development of this book. Richard, thank you for your trust. Also, to Craig Hettrich, thank you for introducing me to Richard.

Annette Schwerdtfeger, my big sister, you edited this manuscript just as you did with my last two titles. I never expected you to take such an active role in my book projects. You consistently notice mistakes that others miss. Thank you for taking the time to read my work and provide such detailed and thoughtful feedback.

John Armato, thank you for your book title ideas as well as the broader discussions we've had on this topic. Karen Coons, thank you for lining up the ABSN interview. Jim Fitzpatrick, Louie B. Free, and Jim Rembach, thank you for having me on your respective TV shows and podcasts. Joanne McCall, thank you for helping me with the public relations effort.

Stephanie Chandler, this is the third book you have published for me. Your counsel and direction are invaluable. Thanks for your recommendations and also for your patience. Writing books wouldn't be as much fun without your input.

George Mason, you are an editing aficionado. I'm so happy that Stephanie recommended you. Thanks for your thoughtful and detailed edits.

Other suggestions and edits came from Alfredo Romero Vega, Amr Selim, Cathleen Hoffman, Chris Van Zeist, Eric Wentworth, Juan Jose Garcia, Louie B. Free, and Mackenzie Singleton. I am grateful for your testimonial quotes and other contributions.

Nadia Flores, thank you for your patience throughout this process. I spent many hours in front of my computer, and that wouldn't have been possible without your love and support.

CONTENTS

WELCOME TO 2020

This is a difficult time. The COVID-19 novel coronavirus pandemic has resulted in an unprecedented worldwide quarantine, and the economic damage will be catastrophic. Unemployment claims are an order of magnitude higher than previous records (set back in 1982), and 40% of Americans have less than $400 in savings (according to a 2018 survey conducted by the Federal Reserve). After just two weeks of quarantine, almost one third of American renters (31%) were unable to pay their full rent (according to the National Multifamily Housing Council).

The retail sector (including companies such as Macy's, JCPenney, and Nordstrom) has been in decline for 20 years already, pushed aside by online platforms such as Amazon. After the quarantine, consumers will be slow to return to their past shopping habits. If you're not leaving your house, there's no reason to wear nice clothes anyway.

Virtual channels will continue to steal buyers from traditional shopping malls. Many of those malls are sitting on prime real estate. Slowly but surely, over the coming years, they will mostly be redeveloped into residential and/or multi-purpose housing projects.

Most non-essential businesses have been closed. According to a 2015 JPMorgan Chase Institute analysis of 597,000 businesses, only half have enough cash on hand to survive a full month without new revenue. The quarantine will last eight to ten weeks at a minimum, meaning many businesses may never reopen. Large companies and chain restaurants may weather the storm, but smaller operations may disappear forever.

Airlines, hotels, tourist destinations, and convention centers are suffering enormous losses, and people will be slow to take trips as they did before, even after a vaccine becomes available. Tourism and corporate events generate huge amounts of commerce, but it will be years before they return to pre-pandemic levels, if ever.

In the end, this pandemic will exacerbate the already widening division between rich and poor. The bottom half of the population will experience severe hardships while the wealthy will live on savings until the storm has passed, and then purchase real estate and other investments at bargain basement prices.

This pandemic is a historical event on a biblical scale. Untold human suffering will ensue. It's all very sad and sobering. But amidst the death and carnage, there are some very real and tangible things that businesses can do to (1) **survive**, (2) **rebuild**, and (3) **thrive** after the crisis is over, and we have never needed business leadership more than we do today.

The only way we can recover from this economic catastrophe is if businesses **survive** the short-term liquidity crisis, **rebuild** their operations to fit new realities, and **thrive** in tomorrow's post-pandemic economy.

Make no mistake: We will see more change in the next 12 months then we saw in the last 12 years. This is a time of incredible change, but change = opportunity. The foundational equation of successful business is to find a problem and fix it, and we haven't had this many problems in a long time.

So, if you're an entrepreneur, business owner, executive decision-maker, or venture capital or private equity investor, you need to look for opportunities amidst the chaos. You need to look for problems and fix them. You need to seize this moment to redefine tomorrow's economy.

This book has ten chapters. First, we need to discuss the current state of affairs and identify risks on the horizon. After that, we'll highlight eight business trends that are accelerating as a result of the pandemic and quarantine. These trends form a convenient acronym:

SALVAGED

S: Self-sufficiency
A: Analytics
L: Liquidity
V: Virtualization
A: Automation
G: Government
E: Exponential Thinking
D: Decentralization

Each trend will be covered in its own chapter. We'll look at the implications of each one, including smaller trends within the larger umbrellas, and offer some strategic questions and tactical to-dos for business leaders to consider.

The last chapter, Chapter Ten, will look at "disruptive innovation" and why it has become so important in today's technology-driven economy. We'll look at some examples and introduce two models to help you anticipate and capitalize on disruptive innovation. Finally, we'll leave you with a strategic framework to navigate your business into the future.

We need visionary leaders. We need bold leadership. As horrible as this situation is, it represents an enormous opportunity for people who can see the bigger picture and envision a better tomorrow. Our world will survive this crisis, and it will eventually become better as a result, but we need your help to get there, so let's get started.

THE SITUATION

The classic 1966 Clint Eastwood western (directed by Sergio Leone) had one of the best movie titles ever: The Good, the Bad, and the Ugly. Let's take a look at our current circumstance with the same three labels.

The Good

The entire world population has one common shared enemy. I don't think that's ever happened before. 7.6 billion people are all confronting the same problem. There are lots of very smart people on this planet, and they're all working on the same challenge. There will undoubtedly be a landslide of creative and effective solutions developed in very short order.

We can't imagine the possibilities today, but the creativity of our global population is undeniable. One need only look at our pre-pandemic world to see the incredible products and services already imagined and created for us all to enjoy. And with today's interconnected online world, good ideas from around the globe will be discovered, developed, and shared faster than ever before.

We have also seen a resurgence of kindness within our communities. People have renewed appreciation of front-line workers including medical professionals, police officers, grocery store clerks, and delivery drivers. Even in a more general sense, we've seen kindness bubbling up all around us.

Canadians started a new trend called "caremongering" as an alternative to "scare mongering." These groups encourage people to share their needs or offer help, allowing those in need to receive support within their own communities. Facebook developed similar functionality to help community members connect and support each other.

There's a distinct sense of shared experience within our communities. People share knowing looks as they pass each other on sidewalks. Empathy and compassion are on display. We all feel the need to acknowledge each other and be supportive. It's been heartwarming to see this spontaneous kindness bubble up, and I hope it remains after the crisis has passed.

The Bad

We'll see headline news of sickness, death, and struggle for months on end. A lot of people are suffering, either medically or financially, or both, and those stories will be leveraged by media outlets looking for clicks and attention. Sadly, they will compete with each other to share the most graphic stories possible, and our population will have to find ways to digest all of that hardship.

This is the unfortunate reality of our "media industrial complex." Media outlets are businesses, after all. Their product is the news, and they'll try to sell it to as many people as possible. We've seen this play out for decades already, but it's gotten worse in today's social media age. As the competition for attention has increased, so too has the media's willingness to share clickbait-driven headlines designed to grab our attention, even if just for a second or two.

The result is that the public is inundated with negative and often graphic news headlines. Most people believe the world is in far worse shape than it actually is. The truth is that the world is getting better, generally speaking, every year, but most people believe the opposite. And today, with a genuine crisis on our hands, the public sentiment has gotten even worse.

The brutal truth is that we're in a very deep recession with incredible levels of unemployment. That reality is being pounded into our heads on a daily basis.

This persistent negativity affects some people more than others, but it affects us all in one form or another. For some, it feels like they're walking through three feet of mud. It's a debilitating sense of sorrow and hopelessness. For others, it makes it difficult to get a good night's sleep. For still others, it fuels mental illness and exacerbates dependencies such as drug and alcohol addiction.

Whether making decisions as a business executive or an individual, we all need to be sensitive to the elevated levels of anxiety within our communities. People will be dealing with all sorts of challenges in their lives, and it will take time for stability and comfort to return.

Approximately 50% of Americans have money in the stock market. When the stock market tanks, you can rest assured that about 50% of the people you come across are experiencing apprehension as their 401K balances drop. Imagine driving down the highway, and half the cars are being driven by people in that situation. You can bet they'll be more agitated as they navigate the traffic around them.

With this pandemic, we do indeed have a huge stock market plunge to digest, but we also have the widespread sickness, death, and financial hardship to consider at the same time. That means the affected percentage isn't 50%, it's 100%. Imagine that same highway where every single car is being driven by someone who is experiencing anxiety in one form or another.

When you consider the implications across an entire population, you begin to see how dramatically life will change as a result. Eckhart Tolle talks about the "collective pain body" in his book "The Power of Now" (2000, New World Library). This pandemic is creating a collective pain body shared by our entire global population. This struggle will leave deep scars in our collective consciousness. As business leaders, we need to be cognizant of that fact.

The Ugly

This situation will bring untold human suffering to our global community, even those blessed with more resources. Nobody will be untouched by this.

A friend of mine owns 35 rental properties in Michigan, North Carolina, and upstate New York. Most would assume he's doing really well, but during the lockdown and quarantine, the employees of his property management providers weren't even coming into the office, so the incoming rent checks weren't being deposited.

Once the dust settled, it became clear that many of his renters weren't paying their rent anyway. Many of his properties still have mortgages, so the hardship of his renters quickly affected his own cash flow. Obviously, this same situation is playing out for countless other rental property investors. The next step is mortgage delinquency, affecting real estate lenders.

Of course, it takes a few months for this domino effect to play out, but it inevitably results in falling real estate values and foreclosures. That leads to short sales and liquidated properties, and we end up in a similar situation that we experienced during the 2008 financial crisis, on top of the broader economic damage from the quarantine.

I suspect things will get scary by the end of 2020, and the fallout could spread far beyond Wall Street. Millions of small businesses will declare bankruptcy. Elevated unemployment, widespread financial struggle, and decimated retail, dining, and travel industries will all be playing out at the same time.

Our central banks have pulled out all of the stops to mitigate the damage, but interest rates are already at zero. The Fed has committed trillions of newly-minted dollars to lubricate financial markets, and that was all within the first month of the crisis. What happens six months later when the wheels start falling off? It's conceivable that the entire credit-based monetary system might fail.

There are a number of ways that might play out. For example, states might start declaring bankruptcy. That's never happened before, but it's possible if the economic domino effect accelerates. For larger states (like New York, New Jersey, Florida, Illinois, or California), it would be similar to bailing out Italy or Spain within the European Union. They're too big. It's just not possible.

When organizations borrow money, whether political entities or businesses, they do so by either selling shares to raise equity or going to the bond markets to raise debt capital. States can't raise equity, so they go to the bond markets, and so do countries like Italy and Spain. When their financial condition deteriorates too much, the bond markets raise interest rates to offset the increased risk.

When Greece's financial crisis began, their interest rate in the bond market rose above 7%. That would dramatically raise their future interest obligations and strangle their annual budgets. As a result, Greece was bailed out by the rest of the European Union, which is the only way they could obtain the necessary funds without paying exorbitant interest rates.

That strategy worked with Greece and Portugal, but those are relatively small economies. If Italy or Spain were in the same situation, there's no way the European

Union could bail them out in the same way. And, by the way, that eventuality is definitely possible in the coming months and years.

Japan has more debt than any other developed country. It's well over 200% of their GDP. So far, they have not met the same fate within the bond markets, largely because of their population's higher savings rate and, more recently, because the Bank of Japan has been printing money and purchasing the new debt as part of their "quantitative easing" program. Although quantitative easing is a relatively new tactic in America and Europe, Japan's been doing it for almost 30 years!

With Japan as a model, it's possible that our government could take on a pile of new debt, financed entirely by the Fed, but the system is bound to break at some point. If and when it does, the first result would likely be a rapid devaluation of the currency, resulting in huge inflation (on imported goods) for domestic citizens, but that is unlikely in the short term.

Our economy has been running on a credit-based monetary system for decades. When Lehman Brothers collapsed in 2008, and the financial crisis moved into full swing, there were real concerns that the credit-based monetary system could fail, but it didn't happen.

Between the $700B Troubled Asset Relief Program (TARP), later reduced to $475B, a series of corporate bailouts, and the relaxed mark-to-market accounting rules approved in March 2009, markets started operating normally again, albeit with much higher government debt balances. Nevertheless, the crisis was averted for the time being.

In 2020, things are both better and worse. Private sector banks are in better shape and have better safeguards to reduce the contagion of a large-scale liquidity crisis, but government debt balances are much, much higher. The Federal debt (including both public debt and intragovernmental holdings) is above $24T in 2020 while GDP was only $21T in 2019, so about 120%, and annual deficits will spike for the next two years at a minimum.

The situation is perilous and could cause unpredictable outcomes. Let's look at a few in a bit more detail.

Possible Sovereign Debt Crisis

Many people believe that unprecedented money printing by the Fed will cause inflation, but that is unlikely in this case. On the contrary, reduced trade, lower demand for oil, and lower oil prices all result in lower inflows of US dollars in emerging economies. Meanwhile, many of those same economics need US dollars to make payments on USD-denominated sovereign debt.

The global economy needs *more* US dollars, not less, but there's no easy way to distribute them. If trade and oil prices remain low, it could cause a cascading debt crisis across emerging markets. The US dollar is gaining value against almost all emerging market currencies (even after the Fed started printing money), exacerbating the problem for foreign borrowers.

Complex relationships behind international financial markets result in unexpected consequences. Money printing is not guaranteed to cause inflation. There are circumstances where it might cause debt *deflation* in global financial markets, pushing the US dollar even higher, and offsetting inflation within US consumer markets.

Furthermore, as just mentioned, the rising dollar could accelerate debt crises for countries holding USD-denominated debt, resulting in a sovereign debt crisis similar to the 1997 Asian financial crisis, except on a much larger scale. Judging from exchange rate trends since March 2020, Mexico, Brazil, South Africa, Colombia, and Turkey would be among the worst affected.

The US dollar has been the world's reserve currency for decades. Today, the pandemic and resulting quarantine is inflicting multiple shocks to the global system. Reduced international trade and collapsing oil markets are causing US dollar liquidity crises around the world, causing the dollar to rise in value, magnifying the debt burden, and causing growth to slow even more.

Money printing will not solve this problem, because the newly minted currency isn't finding its way to the countries that need it. There is no solution for this, at least not that I'm aware of. It's a structural problem, and we'll all find out together how it progresses from here. Suffice it to say, risks are rising.

Every financial crisis is different. You can go all the way back to the Great Depression. Every stock market plunge had a unique cause that had, at that point in time, never happened before. That's always true. If it had happened before, we would've had mitigating strategies to avert the crisis. The only reason these situations spiral into crises is because we're caught off guard.

Expect the unexpected. We have no idea where the current economic shocks will lead. We've never been here before. My objective with this discussion is to heighten your awareness to the possibilities. We will not get through this pandemic without further financial shocks. We don't yet know exactly what they will look like, but I guarantee they're coming.

Everyone worries about the "second wave" of the COVID-19 virus, and it's a valid concern, but we'll also have a few months to plan our response to that possibility. By definition, we will have dealt with the virus already once before. The bigger concern is how the financial shocks play out. Those are far less predictable, because this is the first time we've confronted them.

The European Union

As noted above, the economic fallout from this pandemic could possibly result in the European Union (EU) collapsing as well. I'm not suggesting this *will* happen; I'm suggesting that it *might* happen. Keep in mind that the EU is a monetary authority, not a fiscal authority. That's been the problem from day one. You need both working hand in hand.

When a monetary authority doesn't have any fiscal control, problems are virtually guaranteed. And with the enormous strain caused by this pandemic, and countries like Italy and Spain in severe financial distress, it is indeed possible one of them will either need an enormous bailout, or need to exit entirely. That would accelerate the decline until the whole organization falls apart.

The reason EU officials have been so harsh during Brexit negotiations is that they want to make it difficult for other countries to follow suit. If it's easy to exit the union, other countries will line up to do the same thing. But during this crisis, it may become impossible to stem the tide. And after one country exits, the situation for the remaining countries will become even worse, increasing the incentive for them to exit as well. If two or three go down that road, it's inevitable that the block will unravel entirely.

In September 2019, President Donald Trump said during a speech at the United Nations, "The future doesn't belong to globalists. The future belongs to patriots." It's quite possible that he could be proven right. There's no question that this pandemic, combined with Trump's trade and tariff war, will slow globalization in the near term at a time when protectionist and populist policies were already on the rise.

Populist leaders have gained power around the world; Erdogan in Turkey, Duterte in the Philippines, Chavez (now Maduro) in Venezuela, Bolsonaro in Brazil, Obrador in Mexico, Boris Johnson in the United Kingdom, and Trump in the USA all espouse nationalistic priorities. This pandemic will accelerate the trend towards populist leaders and nationalistic policies.

The pandemic has only fueled existing anti-globalist trends. Countries have made sweeping pronouncements against foreigners, mandated restrictions for international travelers, and even closed their borders. Some of these restrictions will undoubtedly remain after a vaccine has been developed and the crisis is over. Trump's "America first" policies will gain support as will similar policies in other countries.

Supply Chain Shocks

Another area of concern is the global supply chain. Since the quarantine started, we've seen milk being poured down the drain because there was no way to get it to market. Beer producers had their product in kegs (for restaurants), not bottles (for retail consumers), resulting in shortages on store shelves. The oil industry ran out of storage capacity, plunging oil futures below zero as a result. These supply chain disruptions will continue as we reopen our economies.

China went through the pandemic before the rest of the world. During their shutdown, domestic companies saw their Chinese-produced products held up in shuttered factories. Then, when China reopened, Western economies were in the middle of their shutdown. Although Chinese producers were ready to start producing again, their American customers weren't placing orders. These demand shocks ripple through the supply chain until normalcy returns to the market. That could easily take months.

On April 26, 2020, Tyson Foods chairman, John Tyson, published an open letter on their website (and also in full-page ads in the *New York Times*, *Washington Post*, and *Arkansas Democrat-Gazette*) warning that the food supply chain is "breaking" due to plant closures. Tyson and other major producers including Smithfield Foods and Cargill have already closed multiple plants due to COVID-19 outbreaks among employees.

The impact is huge. When processing plants close, farmers from across the nation have no place to sell their livestock, resulting in the "depopulation" of millions of chickens, pigs, and cattle. This is a serious food waste issue, and it's sacrilegious to farming ethics and culture.

It's worth noting that Donald Trump reacted to John Tyson's open letter just two days later, signing an executive order to keep food production plants open. That executive order probably has a few hurdles to cross before it's fully enacted, but it's a good first step. The supply chain has many moving parts, and you can't take one piece out without affecting the rest.

It's difficult to predict where these supply and demand shocks will lead. I'm not suggesting overall food shortages, but there are indeed a wide variety of possible outcomes. Again, expect the unexpected. Lots of well-designed markets and systems are currently in disarray. That creates opportunities, yes, but it also increases the odds of wildly unexpected outcomes.

Social Unrest

By the end of April 2020, the stock market had already retraced 61.8% of the original plunge. We don't yet know if the rally will continue, but it's already quite shocking, given the circumstances. Although the infection curve is flattening, and economies are starting to open up again, we're also processing catastrophic economic numbers with no end in sight. Why is the stock market rallying?

The short answer: The Fed. The Federal Reserve has expanded its balance sheet by more than $2 trillion since the crisis started. Rates have dropped back down to zero, and the federal government has passed another $3 trillion in fiscal stimulus. That amounts to approximately $5 trillion in total stimulus so far, representing about 25% of the US annual GDP.

All of this stimulus travels through a variety of channels, but it usually ends up in the hands of people who own assets such as real estate or stock market equities.

Regular workers receive stimulus checks which they use to pay their rent or mortgage payments. In that case, it took just one step for the money to flow through the hands of average people and back into the hands of land owners.

The Fed agrees to purchase corporate bonds (including junk bonds), and the stock market rallies, assured that any potential corporate bond crisis will be nipped in the bud. Again, in just one step, the stimulus flowed right back to those who own stock market equities.

The stock market has also changed dramatically over the past two decades. The largest companies by market capitalization are almost all technology companies today, and they are less affected by the pandemic than non-technology companies. In fact, as of February 2020, the largest five stocks in the S&P 500 accounted for almost 18% of its market value, the highest percentage in history.

The Wall Street rally is a slap in the face to Main Street workers. The 33 million people newly unemployed are mostly low-wage workers. The businesses that will soon declare bankruptcy as a result of the quarantine are mostly small, privately-held companies. Neither group affects the stock market.

Investors just don't care about Main Street. It's even worse now than it was during the financial crisis, so we can expect renewed tensions between Main Street and Wall Street. Protest movements such as Occupy Wall Street or Black Lives Matter will most likely resurface in the months ahead. The bias towards Wall Street is too pronounced; favoritism towards the rich is too obvious.

We've already seen protests against the stay-at-home orders during the quarantine. The bottom half of our population will soon be experiencing severe financial distress, and the top 10% or 1% or 0.1% will be flying higher than ever. That disconnect will fuel rage and disgust across the population, and it's guaranteed to spill over one way or another.

The root cause of this tension is the widening division between rich and poor, and it will widen even further as a result of our current crisis. There are even structural reasons for this to continue, including low birth rates. These structural dynamics are described in "Capital in the Twenty-First Century" (2017, Belknap Press) by French Economist Thomas Piketty. The division between rich and poor is guaranteed to get wider, and that will inevitably lead to social unrest.

There are many paths that could lead to our social order being seriously challenged, possibly leading to a broader financial collapse. Here are the ones we've mentioned so far:

- States within America declare bankruptcy, requiring federal bailouts.

- Italy or Spain leave the European Union, and the EU collapses.

- A rising US dollar results in sovereign debt crises in emerging markets.

- Supply chain shocks result in food (or other vital goods) shortages.

- The widening division between rich and poor results in widespread social unrest.

What would happen if the credit-based monetary system collapsed? Honestly, nobody really knows. It's never happened before, but it's safe to say that things could get ugly very quickly. Remember Superstorm Sandy? It slammed into the New Jersey coast in late October 2012, and it took less than two days for civilized people to turn into animals, fighting in the streets over food and gasoline. Similar chaos ensued after Hurricane Katrina hit New Orleans in 2005.

There's a common misconception about human nature. Most people believe that we are civilized creatures who act like animals from time to time. That's not true. Humans are *animals* that have learned to act *civilized* most of the time. Civilizations have existed for about 6,500 years, which is a blink of an eye in evolutionary terms. Human beings are animals. We are carnivorous beasts by instinct, but we've chosen to live by civilized rules most of the time. When crises happen, the rules change.

There were already some isolated cases of rioting in southern Italy when the pandemic was first spreading, and protests started across the United States by mid-April. Of course, we had elevated levels of public protests and rioting in countries all around the world before the coronavirus even made an appearance. Protest movements have erupted globally, driven mostly by income inequality, and that will get worse very soon.

Chaos and rioting are difficult to think about. It seems impossible until you find yourself in the middle of a protest. Things happen quickly and often take unexpected turns. Certainly, I do not know what might happen if the credit-based monetary system fails, but it's easy to predict the inevitable winner of that scenario.

Bitcoin and other cryptocurrencies will benefit the most from widespread chaos in financial markets. Seizing credit markets and rapid currency devaluations would explode cryptocurrency valuations. Cryptocurrencies have decentralized architectures, so central banks represent a *centralized* monetary system, and cryptocurrencies represent a *decentralized* monetary system. That's an important distinction, and we'll talk about this more in the chapter on Decentralization.

The Ugly scenario is brutal. Again, I'm not predicting that all of these things will come to pass, but the probability is rising. And if one major deterioration unfolds, the others immediately become more likely.

The Italian economist, Antonio Gramsci, wrote in the 1930s, "The old world is dying, and the new world struggles to be born. Now is the time of monsters." At the time, of course, he was probably referring to emerging populist leaders such as Stalin, Mussolini, and Hitler. There is no evidence that this situation will end the same way, but there are definitely similarities.

COVID-19 Parties

Once economies start to reopen, those who can prove that they have COVID-19 antibodies (they had the disease, recovered from it, and are now theoretically immune to it) will have significant advantages. They will be "safe" to socialize with. They will be at lower risk of endangering those around them.

The extent of this immunity has yet to be scientifically established. There are some who recovered from the disease only to catch it again. At some point, however, some verifiable level of immunity will emerge.

Once that is established, there will be strong incentives for people to catch COVID-19 and get through the sickness as quickly as possible. There are plenty of people who aren't even remotely scared of this virus. They're young or healthy, or both, and they're convinced they'll be mostly asymptomatic if they caught the virus. For them, the benefits of catching the virus, and then recovering, far outweigh the risks.

The downside is that more carriers, even asymptomatic carriers, will predictably lead to more overall infections, affecting people who are much more compromised from a health perspective. That would result in another surge of cases, possibly overwhelming hospitals and healthcare systems. Despite these risks, we can expect stories of people who got together explicitly to catch the virus: COVID-19 parties. The incentive is all too clear.

There are others who feel like the virus is naturally culling the population of old people who already have significant health problems. They believe it's a natural and even positive development, ridding the population of healthcare liabilities, and leaving the rest of us stronger and healthier. Even in my own circle, I know a few people who feel this way, including some who are old themselves.

These are difficult realities to discuss in polite company. Many would be appalled and disgusted at the mere suggestion of these views, but one need only browse social media posts to see examples.

There are only two ways this pandemic will end. The first involves the development and widespread distribution of a vaccine. Between development and distribution, a vaccine is probably a year away. The second involves "herd immunity" within the population. That's the point at which a sufficiently large percentage of people have caught and recovered from the virus, resulting in fewer and fewer transmissions, and eventually stamping it out altogether.

There is already significant online chatter about herd immunity, and it will increase as economies reopen. Sweden is pursuing this already. The incentives are too obvious. As leaders, we need to be realistic about these eventualities. They're predictable.

It's also worth noting that some supplements appear to have efficacy against the infection (although their efficacy has not been reviewed or verified by the FDA). Zinc, vitamin D3, and probiotics are commonly recommended. Also, don't wait until you're sick to begin taking these.

I've been taking all three daily for years. Vitamin D3, in particular, needs time to build up in your system, so it might make sense to proactively include them into your daily routine.

A Better Tomorrow

As awful as the previous discussion was, the economic fallout might nevertheless usher in a new era that operates very differently from our current system. This discussion is pure speculation, but it's worth imagining what that might look like. I spent a fair amount of time describing those scenarios in my pre-pandemic 2018 book "Anarchy, Inc.: Profiting in a Decentralized World with Artificial Intelligence and Blockchain" (2018, Authority Publishing), and I encourage you to read that for more details.

The one word that encapsulates it best is Decentralization. That's also the eighth trend in this book, so we'll discuss it more later, but it represents the largest macro trend encompassing most of the others, either directly or indirectly. And with technology facilitating increasingly decentralized systems, we might soon live in a world with more emphasis on local communities, local cultures, local providers, and local leaders.

Every crypto-enthusiast's utopian fantasy involves a world with fewer political structures, fewer financial structures, and fewer institutional structures. Obviously, if the overarching structures of our economy, including the credit-based monetary system, collapse, it will result in a brand-new system that might easily be built on top of a decentralized blockchain infrastructure.

During the depths of the Great Depression, President Franklin Delano Roosevelt (FDR) began enacting a series of regulations that became known as the New Deal. It encompassed relief, reform, and recovery from the economic downturn, which fundamentally changed the social safety net in the United States. Many of those programs still exist today.

Depending on the scale of the coronavirus-induced economic downturn, and the resulting changes to public sentiment, we may see a whole new batch of regulations enacted in the not-too-distant future, not just here in America, but also around the world. Perhaps Medicare for All will emerge from the rubble, or a higher minimum wage, or free college education.

These are all left leaning socialist programs, but it could go the other way too. We might end up with fewer regulations, no minimum wage, and less bureaucracy.

It's impossible to predict what will happen, or in which direction political solutions will lean. The important thing is to realize that the magnitude of this crisis could easily be big enough to result in significant political changes. We can't seize those opportunities unless we're expecting them. We need to be prepared to have those conversations.

Change = Opportunity

We don't yet know how this will all play out, but we *do* know that things are in flux currently. Imagine that your life and the surrounding economy is represented by 100 blocks. In normal circumstances, 95 of those blocks are nailed down. They're stationary. They're not moving, at least not very much. That builds a sense of certainty and confidence for the people within that community. Only five blocks are in motion.

Today, it's the opposite. Only five blocks are nailed down; 95 are moving. Everything is in motion, and that's very scary for people in the community. It's like being swept away in a raging river. The water is moving too quickly. There's nothing to grab on to. The COVID-19 pandemic threw everything into disarray, and it will take a long time for the new normal to emerge.

The good news is that this same situation creates enormous opportunities for leaders to reshape the new world. 95 of 100 blocks are in motion. That means you have far fewer constraints than you did during pre-pandemic times. People are looking for leadership. People are desperate for solutions and will consider options that they would never have considered in other circumstances. That all spells opportunity to proactive leaders, whether political or in business.

Much of my work as a Business Futurist is on disruptive innovation; how to anticipate it, and how to capitalize on it. Although disruptive innovation has existed for a long time, these days it generally involves new technologies that create new markets with new value networks, displacing established market-leading firms, products, or services. We'll be discussing disruptive innovation in detail in the last chapter of this book.

The COVID-19 coronavirus pandemic and quarantine isn't an example of disruptive innovation, but it's definitely disruptive. By shocking the global population with the dangers of a contagious virus, and by resulting in an unprecedented global lockdown and quarantine, the pandemic has disrupted almost every industry in one way or another, and there are certainly some that may be displaced entirely.

The John M. Olin School of Business at Washington University did a study in 2014. It estimated that 40% of Fortune 500 companies would no longer exist in 10 years. That's a scary proposition. Fortune 500 companies are large organizations with huge numbers of employees, so the disappearance of 200 of those businesses (40% of 500 companies) would have a massive impact on the economy.

The reality is slightly less scary, and actually quite exciting, because 40% of Fortune 500 firms disappearing does *not* mean that 40% of the economy will disappear. If those companies fail, some other new companies will grow dramatically and take their place. These are large markets that have been serviced by established providers for years. Now, over the next 10 years, those incumbents will disappear, leaving massive opportunities behind for newer and more innovative companies to take their place.

Change = Opportunity

When established companies fail, it means new companies will grow. Newer and better solutions will be developed, and the businesses offering those superior solutions will experience dynamic growth to fill the void left behind by old established companies. The pandemic and economic aftermath will accelerate the demise of old-school companies, and that will make this even more exciting for new trail-blazing businesses.

If you can look past the hardship and struggle, this is a very exciting time! Opportunities are around every corner, and people are desperate for solutions. You will only benefit from this situation if you see it as an opportunity. If you look for hardship, you'll find it everywhere; if you look for opportunities, you'll find those everywhere too.

Failure to Adapt = Failure to Exist

Every business will need to adapt to new realities in the post-pandemic world. Those who don't will probably cease to exist. The changes are too profound. Public perceptions will be different, and behaviors will be different too. This circles right back to the analogy discussed above. 95 of 100 blocks are in motion. Everything is changing, and it will continue changing for at least the next year or two.

This is the time of monsters, it's true, but heroes will be made at the same time. Many of the most exciting and innovative companies making waves today were born during the 2008 Financial Crisis and Great Recession. There's no doubt that the most exciting companies of 2025 will emerge from the coronavirus pandemic and economic fallout.

The only thing required to be a leader is to lead. Find a problem and fix it. Lead your customers, employees, suppliers, and channel partners to a better tomorrow. Help reshape tomorrow's economy. Are you a leader? If so, this is your moment to shine. Our economy needs your leadership, and our employment markets need your business model. Embrace this moment, and help our global community get through this crisis.

The Great Pause

Before we dig into the opportunity before us, we should also acknowledge the incredibly unique situation we're currently in. I'm writing this book in early May 2020, in the midst of the quarantine. And although the suffering is real, and anxiety levels are rising, it's also peaceful and quiet outside. The planet is resting.

The freeways, streets, and sidewalks are mostly empty. You can hear birds chirping in the middle of normally-busy city streets. Wild turkeys have been seen playing and exploring empty school playgrounds. Lions have been spotted napping on paved streets in South Africa. Kangaroos are reconnoitering shopping streets in Australia. Seismologists have even noticed that the earth is literally vibrating less than usual, thanks to the inactivity of its inhabitants.

This peace and quiet won't last very long. Governments are in a mad scramble to reopen their economies. The longer they wait, the more economic damage will result. As soon as at-scale testing, contact tracing, and isolation programs are in place, we can expect things to open up again, and then we'll be barraged with intense marketing campaigns to get our lives "back to normal" again.

Take some time to think about the life you used to live, and how you might change your life after the pandemic is over. What brings true joy to your life? What makes your kids laugh? It's quite possible that we revert to simpler routines in the future. It won't be true for everyone. Some people can't wait to get their hectic lives back on track. But on average, across the population, we'll see significant shifts in behaviors.

As a business professional, you should think about that possibility. You should be cognizant of the human yearning for safety and our increased appreciation of simple pleasures. This opportunity will exist only once in our lifetimes, hopefully, and we shouldn't let it pass by untapped. This is an opportunity to reshape our world, rediscover our communities, and repurpose our lives.

The Stock Market

Which industries will benefit from this situation? Which will suffer? One of the best places to look with these questions in mind is the stock market. The stock market is akin to the ultimate sociology experiment. The price volume action of any particular stock, or the market as a whole, is a reflection of every single participant in that market. The sample size is 100%. That is never true for ordinary sociology research.

For most sociological studies, the sample size, N, is usually between 20 and 1,000 participants, and the researchers then extrapolate conclusions about the entire population based on their hopefully-representative sample participants. All of the political polls that barrage our airwaves generally involve 500 or 1,000 phone calls, and the results are published with a plus or minus 3% margin for error, or something similar.

That's not the case with the stock market. In the stock market, the sample size is 100% of the participants in that market (N=100%), and those participants are all placing their bets with real money, so they're making decisions carefully.

When you look at a stock's price chart, you're essentially evaluating a survey of potentially millions of investors (depending on the stock), all placing bets on whether that stock will go up or down in the future. I can't imagine any other situation where you can so easily get advice from so many smart people.

All of these bets play out in the price-volume action for individual stocks, and all the bets of all stocks collectively are reflected in the price-volume action of the market (such as the S&P 500, Dow Jones, or NASDAQ). Every transaction involves one buyer and one seller, and they're all reflected in that price chart somewhere. The volume traded at each price level is reflected as well. It's the ultimate crowd-sourced ranking system for businesses within our economy.

Anyone can easily use a "stock screener" to sift through all publicly traded stocks and search for those trading "at or near their 52-week high." That simple step will immediately isolate the stocks doing well during the current time. Of course, the results of a stock screen like this will change each and every day, but you can check it out any time you please.

The stocks that are benefiting during the early days of this pandemic and quarantine generally fall into five different categories.

- Virtual Work: Zoom, Slack
- Online Entertainment: Zynga, Netflix
- Consumer Retail: Walmart, Costco, Amazon
- Food Delivery: Blue Apron, Chewy
- Pharmaceuticals: Novavax, Moderna

I have no idea if these stocks will continue to do well as the economic fallout takes shape. I am not giving investment advice. I'm simply pointing out that the stock market in general, and individual stocks within the market, are an excellent source of consensus opinions. You can have confidence that the relative performance of one stock to another, or one market to another, represents a consensus of millions of investors all around the world.

This approach will be less useful once we have passed the stock market bottom and resume a healthy uptrend. At that point, the number of stocks trading near their highs will increase, making the conclusions less insightful. During the next few months, as the market tries to digest the magnitude of the economic fallout, it will be useful and I encourage you to check it from time to time, perhaps once each month.

Once we're back to more normal times, change the filter to identify the top gainers for the past 30 or 60 days. You could even limit the filter to industry sectors. That will show you which sectors are advancing more than the broader market. Regardless of what industry you're in, this ongoing awareness will prove useful as you navigate the path forward.

Okay, we've laid a foundation for the rest of this book. We've taken a broad look at the situation and the need for business leadership during this time. We've also highlighted the value of the stock market and its ability to identify leading companies and sectors within the economy. It's time to dig into the eight trends that are accelerating as a result of this pandemic and quarantine.

PANDEMIC TREND #1: SELF-SUFFICIENCY

The first trend that's accelerating as a result of the pandemic is self-sufficiency. Like most of the other trends discussed in this book, it started long ago, but it's accelerating now as a result of our current circumstances. There's always been a contingent of the population that's obsessed with survival equipment, living "off the grid," and relying on nobody but themselves. Their numbers will swell for the foreseeable future.

Solar Power

We're likely to see accelerated adoption of solar panels. These people don't want to rely on the electric grid. They'd rather generate their own power, store it on Tesla Powerwall residential battery units, and possibly even sell their excess power back to the grid for a profit.

People talk about "grid parity." That's the point at which solar power drops below the cost of electricity from traditional fossil fuel sources such as coal or natural gas. Grid parity has already been reached in a number of countries around the world, but the exact cost depends on the alternative resources they have access to. Countries with abundant natural gas reserves will have a lower grid parity cost than countries with limited fossil fuel resources.

There's another level even lower than grid parity, and that's the point at which solar power (from panels on your home's roof) is cheaper than the cost of energy *plus* the cost of transmission from central power providers. Once that has been achieved, it will literally be cheaper to generate energy from your own solar panels than to connect to a centralized electric grid.

The one requirement for off-the-grid living with solar power is battery storage to balance peak energy generation with peak energy usage. Battery technology, like any technology, is evolving along an exponential curve, and the cost is coming down at a fairly predictable rate. Currently, the cost of battery storage per kilowatt hour is dropping by about 12% each year (National Renewable Energy Laboratory).

When calculating grid parity, you have to factor in the cost of battery storage, but you get the idea. Costs are coming down rapidly. The cost of solar panels have dropped by 90% ... just in the last five years! Over the past 30 years, the cost has dropped by well over 99%. In another few years, it will literally be cheaper to live off-the-grid than it will to use centralized power utilities.

It's important to understand the implications of this. Once that cost is achieved, people will switch to solar power en masse. Most electric utility grids will collapse. At a minimum, they will need to be subsidized by local governments, because they will no longer be profitable on their own. It will mark a major milestone towards large-scale self-sufficiency. It will also switch energy generation from a centralized process to a completely decentralized process.

Libertarian Political Views

I know a company that builds underground bunkers, and they're slammed busy right now. People feel unsafe. They want protection from outside risks. A good friend runs a website devoted to backyard chickens, and he tells me that chicken hatcheries are booming. People don't want to buy their eggs at the store. Instead, they want live chickens in their backyard, laying eggs naturally. Gun sales have surged as have sales of ammunition and survival gear. We can expect this trend to continue.

Self-sufficiency enthusiasts generally hold libertarian political views. They want smaller government or no government at all. "Leave me alone!" They tend to have conservative views and identify with anti-establishment populist leaders and nationalistic policies. Many will avoid getting help from government programs even if they're in desperate situations.

These are sweeping generalizations, of course. There are plenty of exceptions, but this description does broadly match the people who have been passionate about self-sufficiency in the past. Now, with this crisis reshaping our economy, more people will be drawn toward these priorities, and their decisions will reflect these views.

"Conspiracy theorists" also fall into this bucket. We've had conspiracy theories for a long time, but there are more and more popping up all the time. Personally, I don't view all conspiracy theories as far-fetched. I view them as normal human behavior.

People want power. People regularly manipulate situations within their sphere of influence in order to maximize their power. Although often destructive and hurtful, that type of behavior sounds quite natural to me.

This isn't true for everyone. Some people want power. Others do not. I have no need for power, for example. I'd rather have love, respect, and choices. I've never yearned for power. It's just not my poison. But many people do, and our social media call-out culture has exposed countless examples.

Keep in mind that conspiracy theories are simply explanations of situations or events that involve multiple people, usually powerful people, conspiring together to unjustly consolidate power, money, or influence. If you remove the word "unjustly," every single corporation would qualify as a conspiracy—i.e., multiple people working together to accumulate profits.

I should emphasize that I don't view conspiracy theories as anything other than the definition just mentioned. I don't use the term in a derogatory way. There are plenty of conspiracies taking place all the time, in which people are conspiring to consolidate power. It is natural behavior for power-hungry people.

The Alt-Right Political Movement

The 2016 election of Donald Trump in America exposed a burgeoning political movement referred to as the Alt-Right. Leading figures within this movement include Steve Bannon who was executive chairman of Breitbart News and later became Chief White House Strategist for President Trump, Alex Jones and his InfoWars platform, and James Corbett of The Corbett Report.

These people (among many others) dig into conspiracy theories with a vengeance, and there are many theories about the true origin of the COVID-19 novel coronavirus, how it was initially handled, the validity of information (or misinformation) provided by nations including China, and the propaganda campaigns after new infections stabilized.

After Trump's surprise victory over Hillary Clinton, millions of people (including myself) scrambled to understand this movement and become familiar with its values. I did the same thing with al-Qaeda after 9/11. I was unfamiliar with Muslim grievances at that time and was unaware of the Sunni-Shiite divide, so I purchased a variety of books and started learning about it.

Today, four years after Trump's election, I've become quite familiar with the Alt-Right movement. There are dozens of media channels, and they have impressive reach. That means these ideas are propagating far and wide within society, so the accessibility to conspiracy theories has never been greater.

Conspiracy theories almost always highlight the dangers of institutions within our society. Examples might include governments, the military industrial complex, churches, business elites, or political parties. The annual World Economic Forum held in Davos, Switzerland, comes to mind. The richest and most powerful people on earth attend the event each year, and conspiracy theories abound.

If societal realities are being manipulated and distorted to benefit a few people at the top, it makes perfect sense that some people would want to check out entirely. So whether these various theories are true or not, the simple awareness and perception of their truth increases the percentage of people who want to live independently.

On May 1, 2020, Elon Musk wrote a barrage of tweets including "Tesla stock price is too high imo," resulting in a $14B drop in the stock's market cap. Other tweets included "Now give people back their FREEDOM" and "I am selling all physical possessions. Will own no house." Musk also included lyrics from "The Star-Spangled Banner."

These proclamations can easily be interpreted as a call to arms for people who believe their freedoms are being infringed upon. Whether that was his intent or not is impossible to know for sure, but these types of statements feed into the desire for self-sufficiency and independence. Many people feel like their freedoms are being trampled on, fueling anti-establishment sentiments.

As business professionals, we should all be aware of these opinions within the population.

- Can your products or services help people live off-grid and become more self-sufficient?

- What about your own business? What changes can you make to rely less on services outside of your control?

Self-sufficiency focused consumers want to deal with companies that have similar values. If your company values align with anti-establishment sentiments, make sure you include that in your marketing messaging.

The Gig Economy

The trend towards self-sufficiency impacts employment preferences as well. Unemployment has risen beyond 20%, and most of those affected were lower-income workers. The vast majority of those people had meager savings to fall back on, so it will be critical for them to find new sources of income quickly.

The gig economy will explode when the quarantine is lifted. Sadly, the increased supply of gig economy workers will drive down the cost of gig economy services, putting downward pressure on income potential. Many of these services offered minimal income potential already; increased supply will push it down even lower.

The best gig economy opportunities include driving (Uber, Lyft, Amazon Flex), freelance virtual assistant (Freelancer, Fiverr), graphic design (99Designs, DesignCrowd), professional services (Upwork, Toptal), specialized consulting (Geniecast, GLG, Clarity), and handyman (TaskRabbit, Thumbtack). All of these platforms will grow.

While the immediate need involves mostly lower-income people, we can expect growth to include higher-skilled workers as well, fueled by the trends towards self-sufficiency, virtualization, and decentralization. I already know a number of highly skilled people who are essentially contract executives, specializing in accounting, marketing, or even CEO. It will soon be possible to run entire businesses with almost exclusively contract employees.

Macro Implications

On a macro level, we need to discuss two other areas: fossil fuel production and automation. These topics may seem unrelated to self-sufficiency, but they both affect our *country's* self-sufficiency in the global economy.

In recent years, US shale oil production (fracking) has skyrocketed, making America a net energy exporter for the first time since the 1970s. Unfortunately, the quarantine has resulted in a huge drop in oil demand and a corresponding collapse in oil prices. At the time of this writing, oil prices are far below the break-even point for shale oil producers. Although oil prices will undoubtedly rebound when the economy is reopened, they may never reach pre-pandemic levels again.

There's an impending revolution in the transportation market, and we'll be discussing it in detail in the Automation chapter, but the short version is that falling costs of both solar panels and battery storage will cause a switch from gasoline vehicles to electric vehicles, and that will reduce demand for oil enough to maintain lower oil prices for the foreseeable future.

The drop in oil prices will force many highly indebted shale producers into bankruptcy, and that will once again increase our dependence on foreign oil producers. That's not necessarily a bad thing, but it directly reduces our own self-sufficiency as a nation.

Secondly, increases in automation result in a smaller impact of wages on the cost of finished goods. Again, we will discuss this more in the Automation chapter, but it's worth mentioning now, because it will reduce the incentives to open offshore manufacturing plants in countries with lower labor costs. Keep in mind that goods produced in Asia need to be shipped across the planet before they can be sold in domestic markets, and that shipping process adds both time and cost to the supply chain.

Highly automated manufacturing processes have very little incentive to be outsourced. There is far less labor involved. As a result, plans for future highly-automated plants will increasingly favor domestic production locations. Unlike the changes in shale oil production, increases in automation do indeed make our economy more self-sufficient over time.

Trade Imbalances

In addition to these two macro trends, we also need to acknowledge the trade and tariff war initiated by Donald Trump in January 2018. It is true that trade barriers favored foreign nations over the United States. Of course, that happened because the USA had many advantages over other nations, including a huge domestic population to sell to. That allowed American producers to achieve efficiencies of scale that were impossible in other countries.

Consider Canada, the country I grew up in. Canada's population is about 10% of America's population, and its people are spread out across a larger land mass, increasing transportation costs. There is no way for Canadian companies to reach the same efficiencies of scale that are available in America. Trade agreements reached in years past reflected those imbalances with higher tariffs on American imports.

I support trade agreements that reflect these inherent imbalances. The American dairy industry, for example, is more efficient than its Canadian equivalent. If there were no tariffs at all, the Canadian industry would wither and die. I'm a supporter of capitalism and free trade, but I also think it's unnecessary to destroy domestic industries entirely.

Trump's trade war with China is different. China has grown from a relatively small economy to the world's second largest economy within 30 years, with very few accompanying updates to legacy trade agreements. In fact, they were invited to the World Trade Organization (WTO) in 2001, giving them more trade advantages, not fewer. As a result, China did indeed have disproportionate advantages when trading goods and services with the United States, and Trump simply strived to rebalance the scale to reflect current realities.

Although the Phase One trade agreement leaves enormous problems unsolved, significant progress was made, and the imbalances are smaller than they were beforehand. That also reduces the incentives domestic companies have to manufacture products in China. The supply chain is shifting. Some of it moved to Vietnam and Thailand, some of it moved to Mexico, and some of it came back home.

These changes will increase the macro self-sufficiency of the American economy over time. None of this will happen overnight. It takes time. But over a decade or two, history will show that our national self-sufficiency grew as a result of Trump's trade war.

These macro trends point in different directions. Falling oil prices will reduce our national self-sufficiency. Increases in automation will increase our self-sufficiency. Trump's trade war will increase it as well. Be aware of these forces shaping our future independence as a nation.

US Presidential Election

Since this book is being written before the 2020 election, some will argue that a Democratic president will reverse Trump's trade policies, but that is unlikely with respect to China. During the trade war, and even more so during the pandemic, it became clear that elites from across the political spectrum and all around the world were equally frustrated with Chinese tactics, and Trump's aggressive actions have unleashed an increasingly united front across the Western developed world.

Politicians and business elites across Europe, the Asia Pacific region, North America, and even the Middle East are sick and tired of unfair trade practices promoted by the Chinese Communist Party, and that cat is forever out of the bag. Many Democratic lawmakers have expressed equally harsh rhetoric against China, so this new consensus is likely to stick.

As business owners or executive decision-makers, you need to think broadly about these micro and macro trends. Consumer preferences are changing, and so are their behaviors. Energy markets, automation, and trade policies are changing as well, and those changes should be considered within your own strategic plan.

PANDEMIC TREND #2: ANALYTICS

We've seen the incredible importance of data as the pandemic spread around the world. Every country handled the situation differently. South Korea, for example, was extremely proactive as soon as they saw the outbreak spreading in China. They put potential testing kits on the fast track for approval by government regulators, allowing them to ramp up testing quickly.

Sweden is also being praised for its approach. Rather than shutting the entire economy down with strict quarantine measures, they decided to keep things open but issue strong social distancing guidelines and ban gatherings of 50 people or more. At the same time, aggressive testing and contact tracing have, at least so far, kept the virus relatively contained.

This was in stark contrast to the bumbling response in America. There was a lack of coordination between federal agencies and state authorities. It took months to ramp up testing, and excessive red tape hobbled every step of the way.

The benefit of testing is the ability to identify positive cases quickly, and then track down others who might have been in contact with the positive cases during the asymptomatic incubation period. South Korea had the testing in place, so they were able to leverage the resulting data. They were able to isolate positives quickly, reducing new infections.

It's important to understand that the incubation period of this virus is what made it so dangerous. It's possible for someone to have the virus without realizing it for a full two weeks before symptoms start to emerge. Apparently, the median incubation period is closer to five days, but even that is scary. It also became clear that many people can have the virus and be asymptomatic entirely, referred to as "silent carriers."

The incubation period for the flu is just two days, and the incubation period for SARS (which started in China and spread around the world in 2002) is between two and seven days. Both are dramatically less than COVID-19, making exponential transmission less likely.

Even with insufficient testing, data still played an important role in America. Hotspots such as New York City and New Orleans monitored emerging cases, allowing them to model future medical equipment requirements. Some models far exceeded the eventual death totals, but those models were nevertheless instrumental throughout the planning and treatment process.

Healthcare Data

Healthcare will transform dramatically in the years ahead, and much of that transformation will be driven by data analytics. Existing healthcare providers are incorporating more data in their business models, but they are also confronting competition from new entrants such as Walmart Care Clinics and Amazon Care, among others. Effective use of patient data has the potential to dramatically improve treatments and health outcomes.

One of the most significant obstacles to innovation is legacy systems. Existing healthcare providers have extensive systems developed over decades in the field. New entrants have no such systems, allowing them to start from scratch and incorporate all of the latest data analytics possibilities. Legacy systems act like an anchor being dragged behind a boat. They were valuable when first developed but slow progress later on.

Teladoc Health is a multinational healthcare company delivering telemedicine and virtual doctor visits, and then leveraging data analytics and artificial intelligence to deliver better outcomes for patients. Healthcare innovators are developing and testing new solutions, and the most effective service models will inevitably spread throughout the industry.

The pandemic has also resulted in accelerated approvals by the Food and Drug Administration (FDA), and that could easily continue into the future as well. The FDA is well known for its tedious bureaucracy, but the urgency of this situation has forced them to accelerate their time-lines. If permanently adopted, that would shorten the time lag between pharmaceutical research and revenue, which would foster increased innovation in the field.

Pharmaceutical companies are facing significant challenges in the next 10 years. Many of the most profitable Rx medications are face expiring patent protection, and the industry is awash with "biosimilar" alternatives as well. On the other hand, major advancements in genome editing and CRISPR-Cas9 technologies show remarkable promise for health outcomes in the future. A shift is taking place, and revenue models will change as a result.

Medical innovations are accelerating around the world, fueled largely by data, and those competitive pressures are affecting our domestic healthcare industry. It's become painfully obvious how different countries responded to the pandemic, either better or worse, and regulatory environments will forever change as a result.

Healthcare academics and researchers are using machine learning to churn through enormous molecular datasets to identify possible medications, not just for COVID-19, but for other medical conditions as well. It's also being used to develop new antibiotics, for example, to stem the proliferation of antibiotic-resistant infections. Data is driving innovation across the industry.

It's worth mentioning that another pandemic is unlikely to hamstring the global economy in the future, at least not to this extent. South Korea had a significant outbreak of the Middle East Respiratory Syndrome (MERS) in 2015 (with 186 cases and 38 deaths). In response, they made important preparations for the next outbreak.

Those preparations paid off handsomely during the current pandemic. They understood the importance of data. We can expect countries around the world to follow suit after today's pandemic-induced economic catastrophe, and health systems will be left better prepared as a result. Accelerated approval timelines, streamlined bureaucracy, and more effective use of data will all play a role in better outcomes during subsequent viral outbreaks.

Exponential Growth of Data

The importance of data has been growing steadily for decades, but the past 10 years has seen an exponential uptick in data collected and data processed. This trend has been fueled by collapsing cost curves. Technology evolves along an exponential curve (exemplified by Moore's Law, for example) and exponential charts famously curve dramatically up and to the right.

People rarely think about the inverse of that curve. The cost of any one capability quickly drops *down* and to the right. The cost approaches zero.

The cost of storing one terabyte of data was about $17,000 USD back in the year 2000. By 2020, the cost of the exact same storage capacity had dropped to just $3, and that same pattern played out for data bandwidth and data processing as well. Those are the three pillars of technology (data storage, data bandwidth, and data processing), and they have all become dramatically cheaper.

The result is a dropping break-even point for new technology projects over time. As the costs come down, it becomes financially worthwhile to accumulate, store, and process more and more data. The birth of "big data" emerged in 2011 and 2012, and the growth rate has only accelerated since then.

The Internet of Things (IoT) was the next logical step. Like technology itself, sensors were becoming cheaper, and operations managers soon realized that they could use sensors for vibration and heat, for example, to anticipate when machines were likely to break down. That would allow them to perform maintenance activities on their own schedule, rather than waiting for the entire production line to shut down unexpectedly.

That became known as predictive maintenance, and it was an early example of positive return on investment (ROI) in the data analytics space. Today, industrial machines are increasingly outfitted with onboard sensors, and one industry after another is optimizing their operations using sensors and data.

Enterprise Software Platforms

The cost to develop new software applications is huge, but proven techniques soon come to smaller businesses at lower cost. Enterprise software providers including enterprise resource planning (ERP) and customer relationship management (CRM) companies incorporate new capabilities into their software platforms. They also provide sophisticated data visualization tools to help business executives monitor key performance indicators (KPIs) and make data-driven decisions. There's enormous power in these systems, but few people take full advantage of them.

I've worked with a variety of ERP companies (including SAP, Oracle, BMC Software, and Epicor, among others), and they all say the same thing. Most of their customers only use a tiny fraction of their platforms' full capabilities. Just like Microsoft Excel, everyone uses it, but few leverage its full capabilities (such as Visual Basic, PivotTables, VLOOKUP, etc.).

The lowest hanging fruit for most businesses is to fully leverage the technology you've already paid for. Get training on the software you're already using. Examine the capabilities of the machines you've already purchased. Explore the reports which are already available. In some cases, the necessary training was included in the price you paid. But even if you have to pay for it, it is money well spent.

A high school friend up in Vancouver is a buyer for a wire and cable distributor, and they started using the SAP platform to manage their operations. My friend loved that platform. It was his thing. He dug into it in the evenings and weekends because he was amazed at its capabilities. He started generating reports comparing data from different areas of the business.

Soon, after sharing a variety of reports with his supervisor, one ended up on the CEO's desk, and he got a call. The CEO was impressed and asked him to incorporate some additional metrics. Before long, he got a promotion and then another. He was providing actionable data with the software that the company had purchased. He was providing strategic value.

As a business professional, you should look for opportunities to exploit the things you've already paid for. With respect to data analytics, there are probably many resources you could tap into now, today, without spending another penny.

- What data is available to you?

- How can you better leverage that data in your decisions?

- Who would be the best person in your organization to spearhead this effort?

Some people are better suited to these tasks than others. You might hate it yourself, and that's fine. My high school friend is particularly well suited to data analytics; he loves it and gets excited about it.

- Who on your team is the best person to exploit these data resources?

Take that person aside and tell him or her about this potential, the importance of it to the future success of the business, and then ask him or her to lead the effort. He or she will undoubtedly feel valued and inspired. Giving someone a challenge results in more engagement, increased productivity, and higher job satisfaction. You might be surprised how much they contribute to your future success.

Data-Driven Optimization

Manufacturing and distribution companies both have enormous potential to optimize operations with data analytics. Look no further than Tesla's efforts to optimize manufacturing processes (building "the machine that builds the machine" with their Gigafactories) or Amazon's efforts to optimize logistics and distribution.

Both are industry leaders and can serve as role models for the rest of us.

"Data is the new oil" is a common phrase in recent years. It's true. Data is the most valuable asset you have. Think about the data you have, the data you could start accumulating, the data you could purchase from others, and the data you could sell to non-competitive businesses. Most companies could track and store far more than they actually do, and there's real value locked up in those opportunities.

Back in the early 2000s, using data effectively was a competitive advantage. It gave you an edge over your competition. But during the past 10 years, using data effectively has become essential just to remain competitive within the marketplace. We've seen the impact that data has had in some industries, so there are now countless ambitious and enterprising entrepreneurs looking for other industries to optimize.

Sand Hill Road in Silicon Valley is often referred to as the epicenter of the venture capital world. Startup founders from around the globe come to venture capital firms to pitch their concepts in search of funding. These pitches are almost exclusively data plays. They are industries where data-based decision-making has yet to be fully exploited, and legitimate opportunities quickly receive funding.

If data is not being fully exploited in your industry, rest assured that it will be soon. 2019 saw more than $130B in venture capital money invested in US-based companies, according to PitchBook-NVCA Venture Monitor.

New startups are nimble and aggressive, so the time is now to step up your data game.

Data-Driven Marketing

Advertising is another field that's been transformed by data. I've done plenty of advertising in my own businesses, and the targeting and analytics are incredible. On Google, for example, I can target all demographic characteristics and location details, but I can also target people's behaviors including which websites they have visited recently. It's all data-driven, and the capabilities are improving all the time.

Mapping prospect behaviors also allows for micro-specific targeting using exclusions from past campaigns. In other words, if you run a campaign where some prospects engage and others do not, you can then exclude one group to better target the other. The initial campaign targets one group, but the follow-up campaign targets two subgroups from the first. After those marketing messages have been delivered, you potentially end up with four subgroups, and then eight.

This is all about "following the customer journey." This phrase has become very popular in recent years, because businesses can follow every individual prospect through the engagement funnel and deliver precise marketing messages at every stage of the sales cycle. The process becomes more intuitive for prospects, and the conversion rate improves as well.

It's also possible to start the marketing funnel on one platform (such as YouTube, for example) and then deliver the next stage on a different platform (such as Facebook). This omni-channel approach creates an immersive and expansive experience for prospects, making the seller look much larger than they might be in reality.

I do this with retargeting. The people who visit my website are then targeted for the next 30 days on Google's Display Network. That means they see my ads on websites like CNN.com and Weather.com for a month after visiting my website. It creates a big impression on people who recently discovered me for the first time.

A friend is the host of a video series about medicinal marijuana. The series is sold online, and their marketing funnel is a case in point for this strategy. On a regular basis, he spends a full day in a recording studio where he records dozens of videos, each designed for people at different stages of the marketing funnel. He has shared the scripts with me, and the level of detail is amazing.

People who engage with this marketing funnel are handheld through the process and given tailored messages along the way. The exclusions and segmentation are impressive, and it's all data driven. The future of marketing is all about these highly personalized marketing funnels facilitated by today's sophisticated advertising platforms.

All businesses can benefit from better marketing, even with offline channels. Displaying signage that matches customer needs is an incredibly simple strategy that measurably improve sales.

- What are your customers' greatest needs?

- What products or services commonly get purchased together?

- What's your most popular product or service? Does your advertising reflect those preferences?

- What percentage of your customers are aware of your full menu of products and/or services?

The easiest sales come from existing customers, so the best place to start is to better understand your customers' needs and then deliver marketing for the corresponding solutions you offer.

It's all about understanding their needs and following their journey, and both are driven by data. Ryan Levesque wrote the book "Ask" (2019, Hay House Business) and created the accompanying "The Ask Method" program to help businesses better understand their customers' needs simply by *asking* them with online surveys. Doing so provides the exact data you need and even guides your future product development process.

Similar data can be accumulated by showcasing three or four offerings on your homepage and then measuring how many people click on each one. Google Analytics is a free and amazingly sophisticated tool for webmasters to monitor and track website traffic. This is another example of freely available capabilities that most businesses fail to exploit. Make sure you have someone on your team who's digging into these data opportunities.

All existing businesses need to exploit data wherever possible. If they don't, other businesses or newly funded startups will come in and disrupt the industry and steal revenue. Customers will spend money with the most sophisticated and intuitive marketers, and the most optimized companies will be able to offer the best prices. The time for "following your gut" is over. Today is about following the data.

The best way to thank an author is to post a review on Amazon. If you enjoyed this book, please take a moment to post a review online. Thank you.

PANDEMIC TREND #3: LIQUIDITY

Cash is king. Cash is survival. Liquidity is essential. The pandemic brought enormous human suffering, but the quarantine and economic fallout brought the cash flow crisis. As mentioned earlier, after just two weeks, millions of people were unable to pay their rent or mortgage. After a few months, the foreclosures and bankruptcies will hit news headlines. After a year, the full magnitude of the financial crisis will emerge from the fog of uncertainty.

The #1 priority for businesses during this first year is simply to survive.

When the quarantine started, my revenue as a keynote speaker immediately dropped to zero. All of my upcoming events were cancelled. Flights were cancelled with ticket prices kept as credit balances with the airlines, to be used against future reservations. Deposits were allocated to future re-bookings at unconfirmed future events. Everything came to a screeching halt.

Similar fates hit millions of people in the hospitality and travel industries. All non-essential businesses were shut down, and the money stopped flowing. Before long, over 30 million people had filed for unemployment insurance, and the initial multi-trillion-dollar stimulus programs were passed in Washington.

My first thought was to look at my bank account balances and see how many months I had in reserves. I have investments too, but they had all experienced huge losses in the initial stock market plunge. We had just witnessed the quickest 30% drop in stock market history. This was not the time to sell investments just to pay bills.

Once my cash reserves and stimulus funds were depleted, it would become necessary to sell stocks, but I was hoping to avoid that if possible. Of course, for many, that wasn't even an option, and the same is true for most businesses.

The reality in business is that this year's profit is this year's profit. Ideally, some of it is left in the company's coffers, but it is often paid out as dividends (or distributions) or spent on stock buyback programs. Next year is left to next year. We all admit that it shouldn't be this way, but in reality, it is what it is.

The result is that most businesses can only survive for a few weeks or months before their cash reserves are fully depleted. At that point, the financial strain flows upstream to suppliers and landlords, and the domino effect begins.

- How much cash do you have on hand?

- How much cash could you scrape together in extreme circumstances?

Start with that, and go from there. When considering next steps for your business, your #1 consideration should be:

- Does it increase or decrease liquidity?

Scrappy Entrepreneurship

When I was young, I always wanted to own my own business. I never did well with authority. I was a lone ranger from the start, but my entrepreneurial fantasies didn't fit the same mold as others. I never planned huge businesses that would change the world. Instead, my fantasies were smaller and more immediate ventures.

- How can I make $500 this weekend?

- How can I make $1,000 next month?

I always thought that traditional business plans were practically useless. They assumed too much knowledge about the unknowable future. As soon as you take the first step, you see new realities and learn more about your marketplace. The only step that's reliable within a business plan is that very first step. All of the subsequent planned steps would immediately need to be adjusted.

That's what happened with this book. I never planned to write it. Instead, a past client asked me to do a webinar to help their members, all business owners, survive the pandemic. I started doing the research and ended up with an outline for nine trends that would most likely accelerate as a result of the crisis.

When I put the first letters of each trend into an online Scrabble word engine, it offered SALVAGED as an acronym for eight of the nine letters. I ended up combining two trends into one, and that turned into the eight trends I focused on. But that still didn't spur the book idea in my head.

The content made sense. With the acronym, it was fairly easy to remember, and it had nice structure to it. I started working on a PowerPoint presentation for the webinar. It took shape nicely, and I wanted feedback from people in my network, so I recorded a screen capture video (using Camtasia software) of the slides narrated by my voice. Once uploaded to YouTube, I shared the link on Facebook and LinkedIn, and also sent it out to an email list of corporate meeting planners.

The video got about 500 views and garnered a number of nice comments. I got about two dozen replies from the email blast, and one was from a producer of a regional media outlet in Atlanta, Georgia. They wanted me to do an interview three days later, and it went well. They asked me to offer three more topics so they could have me on the program again; all good news.

With the strong positive reception in my back pocket, I contacted a public relations firm I had worked with in years past. I told them about the TV appearance as well as the reception it received. I asked if they saw potential to send out a pitch for more TV appearances, and they were enthusiastic.

With their guidance, I recorded three new versions of the original video, and we scheduled the press release for the following Tuesday. It was only on preceding Saturday morning that I thought about writing a book, mostly to support future press releases. And it was only on Sunday that I decided to write the book, irrespective of the press release's reception.

One Step at a Time

You rarely sec Step 2 until you've completed Step 1, and you rarely see Step 3 until you've completed Step 2. You certainly can't see Step 3 or Step 4 when you're first getting started. You need to walk the path for them to reveal themselves. You need to take a step forward. There's no other way. You need to take action in the direction of your goals, and then trust that the next steps will reveal themselves along the way.

I recommend the same approach during this time of crisis and change. Don't try to put a master plan together. Don't look too far into the future. Just look for a problem and take a step towards fixing it. Preserve your cash. See what happens. Evaluate the reception to your first step, and calibrate as necessary. Trust that your next step will become obvious at that point, and keep that process moving forward.

A friend opened a new pest control business last year. When he got his website up and running, he started advertising on five different platforms. He ran ads on Yelp, Thumbtack, TaskRabbit, HomeAdvisor, and Groupon. The first four yielded almost no results, but Groupon worked.

People bought his discounted Groupon deal, and many later signed up for monthly subscription packages. He accumulated a number of 5-star reviews, and some people even found him on the Internet and called him directly. They wanted him to get all of the money from their purchase, rather than letting Groupon keep a percentage.

Seeing the positive results, my friend stopped his other advertising campaigns and reallocated all of those funds to Groupon. His business started to grow and he's now expecting to double his revenue this year, despite the pandemic and quarantine. You rarely see Step 2 until you finish Step 1.

I'm not saying that Groupon is a better platform. We all have different businesses and different markets. We have different strengths, weaknesses, opportunities, and threats. You never know which advertising channel works best for your business until you try all of the alternatives. Take that initial step, and you will quickly see what the next step should be.

As a function of my career as a keynote speaker, I've travelled extensively around the world. I always love visiting cities such as Bangkok, Kuala Lumpur, and Manila. These are scrappy, entrepreneurial cities full of enterprising business people. Everything's for sale! The atmosphere on their bustling city streets reminds me of my own youthful thinking. How can I make $500 this weekend? How can I make $1,000 next month?

Developed Western economies sometimes have too much structure for my liking. It's hard to imagine opening a business, because there are too many hurdles to jump through first. It's intimidating for most people. That's why most settle for a good corporate job. Well, that structure is similar to the 95 blocks I mentioned earlier, all nailed down and stationary. You have to navigate around those blocks to move ahead in the world.

Not anymore! Those metaphorical blocks are no longer nailed down. They're in motion. And while that introduces uncertainty and anxiety into the equation, it also opens up new possibilities and new opportunities. The situation is more fluid now. Yes, our institutions are still there, and most laws remain unchanged, but people are open to new possibilities, and that represents an opportunity for businesses.

Think like an entrepreneur! Think about our economy with that scrappy, enterprising spirit. Try new things while preserving as much cash as possible.

- What's the cheapest way to test a new idea?
- What's the simplest way to test a new business model?

Each step you take will reveal even more ideas to test. Fail fast and fail forward, and iterate toward success!

The imperative to preserve cash will force you to simplify your business experiments, and that will accelerate the iterative process. And the faster you iterate, the faster you discover viable business models.

- What's the minimum viable product?
- What's the minimal viable marketing experiment?

Simplify and accelerate the process. Peter Thiel, co-founder of PayPal in 1998 and Palantir in 2003, is famous for asking: "How can you accomplish your 10-year goal … in the next six months?" This question short-circuits your brain and forces you to think differently about possibilities. Throw out all the preconceived ideas, and start from a clean slate. Test new ideas in the cheapest and fastest way possible, and let that process determine the path forward.

Many businesses will have to look beyond their current bank balances and credit lines to survive this crisis. Call your suppliers and ask for extended payment terms. See if you can outsource certain tasks at cheaper rates. Speak with channel partners to explore joint ventures or sponsorship opportunities. Negotiate with employees to look for temporary cost savings if necessary. The #1 priority is for your business to survive.

You might be surprised at people's willingness to contribute to that cause when spoken to candidly. Obviously, strong ethics are required, but people will help if they trust you. People will help if they feel like they're part of the team. People instinctively want to be part of the solution.

PANDEMIC TREND #4: VIRTUALIZATION

This is perhaps the most obvious of the eight trends. During the quarantine, Zoom calls became ubiquitous. I run a 4,000+ member social group called OC Happy Hour, and I hosted virtual Zoom-based happy hours, joining thousands of other organizers who did the same. I bought Zoom stock and am following others in the same space including Slack and even Microsoft. Wherever possible, the world is going virtual.

The reasons for this are slightly less obvious. During the quarantine, social distancing is essential. Containment is the only tool we have to slow the spread of the virus. But throughout that process, managers and executives discovered what self-employed professionals have known for years: working at home is effective and allows some—not all—people to be far more productive than they are in office settings.

This is even more prevalent for people working in millennial-friendly "flat organizations" where all desks are situated in large open spaces. Facebook's new Menlo Park headquarters featured a huge open space with literally hundreds of desks inside. Co-working spaces and Starbucks coffee shops have similar characteristics. And while they have many pros, including energy and human interactions, they are also incredibly distracting for the average worker.

Working from Home

I've worked from home since 1998, the majority of my working life. It's perfect for me. I haven't turned on my TV in months and I don't get distracted easily. On top of that, I have some definite introverted personality traits and am quite happy staying at home and working on my business. In fact, I probably work more than the average office-dweller, not less.

This isn't true for all people. For some, it's almost impossible to get work done at home. There are too many distractions, and there's a bunch of food in the fridge too, making weight gain a common side-effect. I'm not suggesting that working from home works for all people, but there's a sizable percentage that prefer it. They will increasingly get their way with their respective employers.

With the pandemic spreading in the background, minimizing human proximity is essential. We've already seen plexiglass dividers popping up across the retail sector (including grocery stores, Costco, and the post office), and into office environments as well. People need to feel protected, and transparent plexiglass dividers reduce human proximity without making people feel like they're stuck inside a box.

In the future, productivity and reduced costs, along with *fear* of another pandemic, will propel the trend forward. But it's not just our work that will go virtual. Events, education, and activities will do so as well.

Most first-time users of Zoom are impressed with the level of engagement the platform delivers, but long-time users realize that it's still a far cry from actual in-person events. Dogs barking, kids crying, and garbage trucks outside, beeping in reverse, make it difficult to listen intently to the person speaking. And for that person trying to communicate with his or her audience, it's almost impossible to stay on message when watching distracted people on live video feeds on your screen.

The point is that today, in-person events still have value. Engagement levels are far higher, but there are other technologies that will fix that problem in the future. Virtual reality, augmented reality, and mixed reality all promise to create more dynamic virtual environments for us to explore together.

Virtual Reality

Although no VR headset has yet achieved broad market adoption, it's inevitable that one version or another will hit critical mass soon. My guess is that some famous online personality, perhaps a YouTube celebrity, will one day be photographed walking down the street wearing a VR headset, and that will spur a buying frenzy among young people, and it will spread from there.

Clearly, there also needs to be a critical mass of content (games, experiences, virtual meeting places, etc.) and a sufficiently low price point to be accessible for ordinary people in order for this frenzy to materialize, but those trends are already in place, and their convergence is inevitable sometime soon.

Microsoft was recently awarded a $480 million order from the Department of Defense for augmented reality headsets. That's a leading indicator for the retail VR revolution. Presumably, tens of thousands of young soldiers will be trained on these new devices, and their familiarity with the technology will seep into the broader market. Capabilities will increase, costs will drop, and the revolution will begin.

To simplify the discussion, I'll refer to virtual reality, augmented reality, and mixed reality collectively as virtual reality or VR.

As soon as VR headsets gain broad market adoption, we'll witness a new form of marketing to emerge with record speed. Every large business-to-consumer (B2C) company will scramble to create free VR experiences on their websites, all in an attempt to engage potential customers and build brand awareness.

Ferrari might build an experience where people can race exotic cars through insane racetracks. Coca-Cola could create one involving polar bears in an artic setting. Carnival Cruise Lines may have one where people can simulate bungee jumping off the side of the ship. Disney might have a virtual jungle safari in The Lion King's Pride Lands, complete with Simba and Mufasa to interact with.

With increasingly immersive and amazing experiences freely available online, people (mostly kids at first) could potentially spend all day indoors, hooked up to their headsets, exploring one experience after another. We've all heard stories about kids playing video games for literally days on end, eating almost no food, drinking almost no water, and doing zero exercise. Sadly, these stories will become more common after VR goes mainstream.

From an employment perspective, this will create enormous demand for VR animation specialists. From a small niche industry today, a massive marketing machine will emerge with tens of thousands of VR experience designers, creators, animators, and producers. These are jobs of the future.

- Can your business contribute to this impending job creation?

Imagine attending a virtual conference where you walk through the convention center hallways and interact with other avatars, people whom you might recognize from past meetings, and have instant access to all of your past interactions to support you in this most recent encounter. Gamers are already familiar with these types of online environments, and they can attest to the difference it makes. With VR technology, virtual events may indeed rival the engagement levels of in-person events.

Of course, this all has pros and cons. VR experiences and events will be amazingly immersive, engaging, and entertaining, but they will also give people an incentive to unplug from the real world entirely. This will bolster the trends towards self-sufficiency and decentralization.

As mentioned above, it will also result in people spending more time in virtual worlds.

"The Matrix" was one of the most popular movies of 1999. The underlying premise is that human beings are being harvested for their energy, with each individual living within a cocoon while experiencing their lives entirely within a virtual world. The assumption, of course, is that these humans were pulled into this dystopian future against their will.

The truth is that we're running towards that future as fast as we can! Technology will soon deliver virtual worlds that materially outshine the real world, and an increasing percentage of people will happily pick those utopian options. For obvious reasons, virtual experiences will be most attractive to people with unhappy lives, but the trend will increasingly supplant happy lives too as virtual worlds improve.

VR headsets dramatically improve online experiences. They do an impressive job of eliminating distractions in the room around you, and that instantly leads to higher levels of engagement. They help users make the leap from their current reality into the virtual world. There are even gloves and entire body suits available to simulate virtual experiences in more tactile ways.

Virtual Worlds

Most people have heard about Second Life before. It's a virtual online world launched in 2003. Within 10 years, it had over one million regular users (called residents) who created their own avatars, built structures, explored the virtual world (called the grid), and interacted with each other. Many corporations even created structures within Second Life to engage with its users.

With VR technology on the rise, VRChat was launched in 2014 and provides similar functionality as Second Life along with virtual reality capabilities. To be clear, you don't *need* VR equipment to explore VRChat, but it dramatically improves the experience. Starting on April 29, 2020, and continuing for 12 days, the platform hosted the world's largest virtual expo called Virtual Market 4 (or Vket4).

The expo features thousands of props, accessories, avatars, and building parts created by more than 1,400 artists, and sprawling across 36 worlds, all filled with virtual booths to explore. Vket4 is an excellent model to follow for a preview of future events. Similar to Second Life, human creativity is on full display, and events that fall short in the creativity department will attract fewer participants than those with thriving creative ecosystems.

In the offline world, the annual Burning Man festival in Black Rock Desert Nevada attracts tens of thousands of participants each year, and creativity is the hallmark of its appeal. Human creativity is truly boundless, but it's only unleashed when open participation and co-creation is encouraged. That was true for Second Life as well, and it's now playing out again on VRChat.

As a business leader, regardless of your industry, the time may be near to purchase a VR headset yourself. Oculus Rift and HTC Vive are both good options. Allocate some time to explore virtual worlds. It will give you an idea of what's coming. Virtual experiences are incredibly immersive and engaging. It's not hard to imagine a not-too-distant future with far more options than we have today.

Moderation is key, and most people will keep their virtual adventures in check. The point is that engagement levels will continue to improve within virtual environments, and that will accelerate the trend towards virtualization. Zoom, Slack, GoToMeeting, Webex, and others will incorporate new capabilities as technology allows, and more and more offline events, education, and activities will move online.

Interestingly, virtual work will reduce the appeal of major urban centers such as New York City and San Francisco. Decentralized management teams make other locations more attractive. Meanwhile, population density, shared public transportation networks, and congested living environments increase the risks of viral transmission.

Large cities will always have an appeal. The glitz and glamour are difficult to resist, especially for young professionals. I'm not suggesting these cities will see population declines, but it's very possible that smaller cities become more attractive alternatives, relatively speaking.

Commercial real estate will suffer. Many companies are already planning to reduce office space. Since the quarantine started, Google's parent company Alphabet, for example, has already backed out of deals to acquire more than two million square feet of office space, including the largest deal ever negotiated in the San Francisco Bay Area. Working at home works, especially for white collar knowledge workers.

Real estate values are generally a lagging indicator of the economy. That means they generally drop *after* the economy bottoms, not before. It takes time to make these types of changes, and commercial real estate almost always involves five or 10-year leases. That means commercial office space rates will probably drop in 2021.

These predictions are never guaranteed. After 9/11, industry experts predicted that leasing rates in tall skyscrapers would fall, but they never did. Only time will tell if this latest situation has a more lasting impact on corporate behavior, but office space is a major line item for most companies, so that's a significant incentive for lasting change to occur.

Virtual Influencers

Virtualization has affected marketing in some surprising ways. Social media platforms such as YouTube, Instagram, Twitch, and Tik-Tok have prompted the emergence of influencers with huge followings. Joe Rogan, Dan Bilzerian, Kim Kardashian, Kylie Jenner, Tim Ferriss, Cristiano Ronaldo, and Selena Gomez come to mind.

Today, a number of *virtual* influencers have garnered impressive followings as well. Lil Miquela, KFC's virtual Colonel Sanders, Yoox, Noonoouri, and Shudu are leading examples. These avatars are created by corporate marketing departments and have significant advantages over real people. Their entire existence can be perfectly crafted to reflect the company's values, and you don't have to worry about embarrassing mistakes or old photos or comments that can destroy public perception in today's reactive "cancel culture."

The success of these influencers depends on the personalities they're created with and the content they share. Even with real humans, some people are far more clever and entertaining than others. Every influencer, whether human or virtual, has its own voice, its own opinions, and its own personality. From a marketing perspective, it's an exercise in character development, and creativity and humor play central roles.

We will see more virtual influencers in the future. Some will be created by individuals while others will be corporate creations, but some will become digital celebrities, and they will most likely be managed by entire teams of writers, PR experts, fashion specialists, graphic designers, and animators. It wouldn't surprise me if some eventually want to run for political office, requiring courts to rule on their eligibility.

Robotic Sex Dolls

We can expect virtual companions to proliferate as well. Already today, in Asian countries such as Japan, robotic and virtual assistants have gained traction. These companions may be strictly virtual, but they will also be available in physical forms. A thriving industry of full-size, anatomically-correct robotic sex dolls is gradually incorporating technology to make these sexual companions more appealing.

Companies such as RealDoll, YourDoll, and LumiDolls are building increasingly realistic dolls for individuals and brothels alike. These dolls are gorgeous, catering to every possible fantasy and fetish. Large breasts, tiny waists, beautiful faces, and thick shiny hair are all easily created. The latest iterations are heated, self-lubricating, and even provide verbal responses, all driven by artificial intelligence and socialbot technologies.

For those who have limited sexual options in the real world or who have fantasies that aren't easily satisfied with human women, robotic sex dolls offer an attractive no-hassle alternative. These trends are disturbing and dangerous, but they are unfolding right in front of our eyes, and we need to confront the implications for human relationships and sexuality.

There is a deficit of 30-million women to men in China, largely due to the one child policy. A close friend adopted two Chinese girls, as did millions of others, leaving a shortage of women in China itself. That means 30 million Chinese men will be unable to secure female relation ship partners. Incredibly, there is an even bigger deficit in India, 40 million, so that totals 70 million between those two countries alone.

This is an enormous market with enormous profit potential. Sex doll brothels are opening around the world (including South Korea, Moscow, Barcelona, Torino, Houston, Toronto, and Paris, among many other cities), and in many cases, the sex dolls are more popular than the human women.

Compare this business model with the chatbot "robotic companions for seniors" market. Robotic companions for seniors may replace a few salaries, and they may even charge some sort of monthly subscription fee, but the revenue opportunity pales in comparison with the robotic sex doll market, where dolls can be rented out by the hour. And since the financial incentive is significantly greater for sexual companions, it's only natural that development will advance more quickly in that area. Entrepreneurs already see the opportunity. This will happen quickly.

The impact of this inevitable trend will spell trouble for traditional relationships, and women in particular. There are already a host of unrealistic expectations placed on women by our misogynistic male-oriented society (be beautiful at all costs) and women will soon have to compete with sex dolls with perfect bodies and zero emotional baggage.

There are immense implications for society. It's difficult to predict exactly how the situation will evolve, but the trends are easy to see. Prostitution is the oldest profession in the world, but sexual relationships touch us all. The trend towards virtualization will introduce non-human competitors to that marketplace.

Virtual Companions

Cinematic and television depictions of the future are powerful influencers in the direction of technological development. These depictions are generated by incredibly creative writers, but the resulting movies and TV shows powerfully influence future development. Shows such as Star Trek and The Jetsons have directly inspired countless technologies that are commonplace today.

The 2013 movie "Her" depicts a man who falls in love with a playful and sensitive virtual operating system named Samantha. Movies such as "Her," "Ex Machina," and "I, Robot" will impact future iterations of virtual companions. Sooner or later, something will be created that achieves broad market adoption and becomes commercially profitable, and the market will then explode as competitive forces accelerate the development curve. Of course, Siri, Alexa, and Google Assistant are early pioneers in that space.

The ultimate success of these companions will require smooth conversational speech capabilities. The Turing Test attempts to measure a machine's ability to interact in a way that is undistinguishable from a human. Modern chatbots have already passed the Turing Test in text format, but spoken speech (socialbots) is a more difficult medium.

Google's Duplex platform uses artificial intelligence to make restaurant and salon reservations over the phone using socialbot technology. Search for "Google Duplex" on YouTube to see an amazing 2019 demo when the technology was first showcased in public. The resulting "conversation" between the system and an unsuspecting human operator is completely indistinguishable from that of a regular human interaction.

Over time, these systems will continue to improve, and they will then become more attractive to those who may currently live lonely lives. Social media has already resulted in higher levels of loneliness and depression, so these new technologies may satisfy the need for companionship while simultaneously isolating us even further from other people.

The damaging psychological effects of social media are discussed in more detail in the Decentralization chapter.

This is a paradox of technology. It drives us apart from each other. Already today, we're all insulated by a thick blanket of technology, reducing the direct, unfiltered interactions we have with other people. Then, in response to the resulting loneliness, technology comes to the rescue, exacerbating the underlying problem.

We've already seen elevated levels of social anxiety in our youth, because they're not used to interacting directly with their peers. We don't yet know how that story will end, but technology is guaranteed to play an increasing role in our lives, and direct face-to-face interactions will become less common.

Virtual Education

Education is another area that will increasingly go virtual. With schools closed down during the quarantine, kids have been forced to continue their education using online learning platforms. We have a six-year-old boy, and it's been fascinating to see the tools he's been given by his teachers. In our case, Freckle Math, Prodigy, Kodable, and Lexia Core-5 come to mind, but there are many others.

These platforms monitor students' learning in real time. If mistakes are made, the platform automatically redirects them to subroutines designed to help them learn the material better. Then, once they've demonstrated that they understand the concepts, it brings them back to the primary lesson plan. The result is that testing is no longer required.

The question is no longer, "What score did you get on the test?" Instead, it's simply, "What level are you on?" This 'adaptive learning' technology allows students to learn at their own pace while lowering anxiety and eliminating the stigma of low test scores. It also makes it easier for smart kids to skip grades. If they can blaze through the levels, there's no reason to slow them down.

These educational platforms aren't suitable for all students. There are some who have special needs beyond the available subroutines. Others need more human interaction and get bored and/or depressed with online learning. These technologies will never satisfy 100% of student needs, but they're proving effective across the population, and they'll undoubtedly get even better in the future.

Gamification of educational platforms is another fascinating innovation. In Freckle Math, students are given plain piggy avatars to represent themselves within the class. Each student can see the avatars of all their classmates when they log on. After completing different sections, they receive tokens that they can spend on accessories for their piggy.

There are sunglasses and t-shirts and funky haircuts. Students can select different backgrounds and extras like game console controllers. All of these selections cost different numbers of tokens, so the extent of avatar customization reflects the student's achievements within the learning platform.

Our six-year-old always talks about his classmates, and we know there's a girl who is always at the top of the class. Sure enough, in Freckle Math, her avatar is decorated with every possible accessory, and many others are hot on her tail. This all creates a sense of competition between students, and they strive to out-learn each other over time.

The Khan Academy has also received considerable exposure and achieved considerable success. It was founded in 2008 by Salman Khan and delivers free educational resources for learners. Their resources are translated into 36 different languages and benefit millions of students each day.

Practice exercises, instructional videos, and personalized learning dashboards allow students to learn outside of the classroom and progress at their own pace. Adaptive learning techniques are used to identify student strengths and learning gaps, increasing comprehension and retention.

Virtual Adult Learning

These virtual learning technologies will inevitably be incorporated in adult online learning platforms too. We're starting to see the impending education revolution coming into focus. It's been a long time coming! The insanely-expensive existing education system (including Ivy League universities and colleges) is ripe for disruption, and these advancements in childhood education will creep into their domain in the years to come.

With a shortage of skilled human talent, particularly in the STEM (science, technology, engineering, and mathematics) fields, we've already seen companies (including Google, Apple, Microsoft, and others) develop their own in-house training programs. These companies can then hire primarily on attitude, not just aptitude, and develop employee skills internally.

The profit motive guarantees that these internal training programs will incorporate every strategy that has proven effective within online learning platforms. The coming education revolution will be led by these corporate training programs, not by traditional colleges and universities. Over time, stories will surface of high school graduates who built successful and high paying careers as corporate employees, all without college degrees. Those stories will undermine the traditional college track for future high school graduates.

History shows that technology disruptions can turn industries upside down within 10 years. Once mostly-virtual corporate training programs hit critical mass, future high school grads will abandon their college ambitions en masse. We just need a few of those success stories to hit the headlines, and market forces will take care of the rest.

Virtual Healthcare

Healthcare is also destined to adopt increasingly virtual channels. With a highly contagious virus running wild across the globe, it makes more sense than ever. I've had two virtual doctor's appointments during the past month, and they are easily as effective as in-person appointments.

Companies such as Teladoc Health (mentioned in the Analytics chapter) have built an entire business model on virtual appointments in combination with data analytics and artificial intelligence. They also license their proprietary platform to doctors outside of their network. Customers rave about their services, and their approach will undoubtedly flourish in the post-pandemic world.

Strategic Questions

Work will go virtual. Events will go virtual. Companionship will go virtual. Education will go virtual.

Healthcare will go virtual. People will have much more screen time in the future, so here are a few strategic business questions to ask:

- How can your products or services help people thrive in virtual environments?

- Can you sell things within those virtual environments?

- Can you train people to navigate virtual environments more effectively?

- What about companies? Can you help them develop virtual training programs?

- Can you develop your own virtual training program?

PANDEMIC TREND #5: AUTOMATION

The trend towards automation started 100+ years ago. Henry Ford's production lines were early iterations, and the trend has been accelerating ever since. Now, with a new incentive to minimize human proximity, the trend will accelerate even more. We've all heard of robotic process automation (RPA); that's going to become a core business objective moving forward.

With the top post-pandemic priority focused on liquidity and cash flow, business executives need to balance the lower per-unit costs of automated systems with the capital investment required up front. That requires a system of prioritizing investments that optimizes outcomes.

3D Printing

3D printers have played an interesting role during the crisis. Shortages of personal protective equipment (PPE) led builders, engineers, designers, and enthusiasts to use 3D printers to create ventilators, face masks, and nasal swabs. The best designs were widely shared, and a global movement was born.

Different technologies offer different benefits. 3D printers are highly inefficient compared to injection molding machines; however, one hallmark of 3D printing is that it facilitates rapid, low-cost prototyping, which in this case allowed for immediate production until injection-molding tooling could be created and high-volume production ramped up. This crisis showcased the value of 3D printers, and we can expect the technology to propagate over time.

Automating Repetitive Tasks

Of course, the focus needs to be on tasks currently done by humans. Can those tasks be automated in the future? There are a number of models you can use to structure your thinking within this topic. The noted marketing and technology consultant, Shelton Leigh "Shelly" Palmer offered one I'm particular fond of. Once we focus our understanding of automation opportunities, we can figure out where to invest first.

Palmer's model, broadly speaking, is based on the economy having two primary job categories: manual jobs and cognitive jobs. Manual jobs are often referred to as blue collar jobs, and cognitive jobs are white collar jobs. Within each category, there are repetitive tasks and non-repetitive tasks, which results in four buckets: manual repetitive, manual non-repetitive, cognitive repetitive, and cognitive non-repetitive tasks.

The manual repetitive tasks will eventually be replaced by robotics, and the cognitive repetitive tasks will be replaced by algorithms. Many of these repetitive tasks have already been automated, of course, but there are still plenty more waiting in the wings. We don't know exactly *when* each individual task will be automated, or *how* they will be automated, but we can expect it to happen at some point down the road.

You can refine your expectations (and, hence, your focus) further by sorting the repetitive tasks by their respective levels of complexity. Technology is climbing a ladder of complexity. It's able to handle more and more complex tasks as time goes on. Machine learning and artificial intelligence are examples of increasingly sophisticated levels of complexity. It makes sense that the least complex tasks will be automated first, and increasingly complex tasks will be automated later.

The result of this thought experiment is a list of repetitive tasks, sorted by their likely order of automation. The assumption is that it's a lot easier to find something when you know what you're looking for. The purpose of this exercise is to focus your mind on specific outcomes. Doing so will increase the odds that you find solutions early.

Every time we go to a grocery store or Costco, we see the growing availability of self-checkout kiosks. This is just one more example of repetitive tasks being automated. MacDonald's stores now have large touch-screen order kiosks, and similar technologies are popping up everywhere. These kiosks make it unnecessary for customers to interact directly with employees, and that objective is paramount today. At the same time, we should note that there are more than 3.4 million retail cashiers in America.

There are many reasons to automate repetitive tasks. Although capital investment is required, it will reduce per-unit overhead after the breakeven point has been reached, increasing overall efficiency. But with the pandemic still in full swing, another reason is to minimize human proximity. This imperative will subside after a vaccine is developed, but the trend in this direction will continue.

Non-repetitive tasks will define the jobs of the future. Manual non-repetitive tasks might involve agility, coordination, or athletics. Cognitive non-repetitive tasks might include creativity, negotiation, emotional intelligence, or teaching. The tasks that are most difficult for automated systems are those that involve fundamentally human capabilities such as empathy, regret, shame, and love.

Repetitive and non-repetitive task buckets are not clearly delineated from one job to the next. Even as CEO or an executive decision-maker, you may have some repetitive tasks within your own job description, so include those in your list. Ask your team to make lists of repetitive tasks as well, including those within their own jobs. Ask them to sort their lists by the level of complexity. Have someone combine everything into one master list.

Conscious Awareness

When I did my TEDx Talk on "Learned Intuition," I discussed the fact that we humans are only consciously aware of a tiny percentage of our observations. In any given setting, among our five senses, we make as many as 10 million observations, but our conscious mind can only keep track of about 40. That means 99.9996% of our observations are never consciously contemplated.

Our focus plays a huge role in our interpretation of reality. When I first moved to California (from Vancouver, Canada) in 1998, I bought a dark green Volkswagen Jetta. For the next two or three months, I saw other Volkswagen Jettas everywhere I looked. Many were dark green, just like mine. They were everywhere! Of course, they were always there, but I had never noticed them before.

We notice the things that align with our mental focus. That's the underlying reality behind affirmations, gratitude journals, and visualization. They hone our focus on positive outcomes, and that directly affects the things we see in the world around us. The Law of Attraction suggests that this phenomena is a result of magic or divine intervention. The reality is that it's mostly a function of mental focus and probability. Either way, it can have truly magical effects on your life.

The repetitive task exercise above does the same thing. It puts structure around the topic and leaves you with a list of possible future outcomes (the automation of repetitive tasks). That simple exercise will increase the odds that you'll find beneficial solutions quickly. Revisit your master list of repetitive tasks once each quarter to cross off the tasks you've been able to automate since your last review. This process will remind your subconscious mind to look for more solutions.

Social Distancing and Germophobes

The fear that's emerged as a result of this pandemic is real. There's always been a segment of our population who identify as "germophobes," and that percentage has now increased dramatically. Most of us know at least one or two people who either got sick from the virus or even died from it. Personally, my brother has it, my cousin died from it, and a good friend had it as well. Across the population, that heightened fear will result in new behaviors and different comfort levels.

More people will wear face masks in the future, and some form of "social distancing" will remain after the virus has been stamped out. Whether working at their jobs or socializing with friends, many people will expect more space in between them and their colleagues. That means all businesses will need to accommodate those preferences.

Capacity restrictions for rooms, restaurants, event venues, and elevators will be reduced. Guidelines for "acceptable" distances between people will change. People who are sniffling or sneezing will not be tolerated as they were pre-pandemic. Technology is destined to play a role with all of these new restrictions and guidelines. We're likely to see an acceleration of drone technology adoption, for example.

Even now, in the middle of the quarantine, the Mayo Clinic in Florida started using autonomous vehicles to deliver testing kits. Robots were used in both Chinese and Italian hospitals to deliver meals to COVID-19 patients and check vital signs. Delivery drones, whether on city streets or flying through the air above, will proliferate. Regulators will have a renewed sense of urgency to pass legislation allowing these technologies to deploy.

Autonomous Vehicles

Autonomous vehicles deserve more discussion. Most people have no idea how far the technology has progressed, and how soon autonomous vehicles will be driving on city streets. The progress is fueled by massive amounts of data and "fleet learning" from vehicles within the network.

When Tesla first introduced their autopilot feature in 2015, the necessary hardware was already installed on tens of thousands of vehicles. Tesla had been installing the hardware on vehicles for quite some time before the announcement was made. As soon as the news hit the airwaves, therefore, tens of thousands of Tesla owners could immediately start using the feature.

Many stories have emerged where Tesla cars were initially making mistakes while in autopilot mode, perhaps incorrectly taking an exit ramp or struggling with tight corners, but the drivers who experienced these errors reported that their cars soon "learned" to handle those situations correctly. But it wasn't just those few isolated Teslas that improved from that learning process. *All* Teslas improved at the same time!

This is referred to as fleet learning, and it's a major driving force in today's venture capital circles. It means that individual experiences from each person on the network are uploaded into the cloud (an enabling technology) where the problems are solved, and then the fixes are deployed network wide. That means the rate of improvement is a function of the number of people on the network and the number of different situations they experience.

At the time of writing this, Google's Waymo has accumulated about 20 million miles of autonomous driving data. Tesla, by contrast, has accumulated over two billion miles of data! That gives them an enormous advantage when developing the artificial intelligence required for Level 5 autonomous driving. Data is the #1 requirement for machine learning systems.

Uber has also accumulated a ton of data. It's different data than Tesla's, but it is data nevertheless. China's Uber equivalent, Didi, has accumulated a huge amount of data as well. Inevitably, it's a race for data, and the pace of innovation is accelerating, but that's only half the story.

Electric Vehicles

The other transformation taking place in the automotive sector is the transition from gas vehicles to electric vehicles, and that will disrupt the supply chain a lot more than autonomous driving. The average gas vehicle has about 2,000 moving parts. By contrast, the average electric vehicles has less than 100, and some of them don't even touch each other. That's a 95% reduction in moving parts!

Electric motors are much simpler than gas motors (internal combustion engines), so the maintenance requirements are much lower. That's why Tesla has proposed million-mile drive train guarantees for their Tesla Semi trucks. Electric vehicles will result in a dramatic simplification and contraction of the automotive supply chain and after-market service provider markets.

The most expensive single component of an electric vehicle is the battery, and we've been seeing the cost structure of batteries drop by 12%+ annually in recent years. With the sector growing, enormous investments are being made in battery development, further accelerating the cost curve reductions.

If current trends continue, we can expect unsubsidized electric vehicles to be less expensive than gas vehicles by 2023, and that doesn't even consider the fact that electricity is 90% cheaper than gas on a per-mile basis! It doesn't consider the lower maintenance requirements either. That means electric vehicles will have a lower overall cost-of-ownership by 2021 or 2022.

We have a convergence of trends in the automotive sector. Within two or three years, electric vehicles will be cheaper to buy, cheaper to fill up (recharge with electricity), and cheaper to service. By 2025, if not sooner, it will no longer make financial sense to purchase gas vehicles. The automotive sector is nowhere close to prepared for this monumental shift.

In September 2019, Amazon announced that they would be purchasing 100,000 electric delivery trucks from US electric-vehicle startup Rivian, roughly doubling the total number of electric commercial trucks in all of Europe and North America. This is a glaring leading indicator.

Amazon made this decision because electric trucks will save them money. Countless other companies will make the same decision within the next few years. Electric vehicles will be cheaper to own and operate. It's as simple as that.

Transport as a Service (TaaS)

Many millennials in urban environments have decided *not* to buy cars. Uber and Lyft are cheap and require no insurance premiums or parking fees. Meanwhile, about 75% of Uber fares go to the driver. As soon as Level 5 autonomous driving is approved by regulators, Uber has a huge incentive to use Wall Street money to buy hundreds of thousands of autonomous vehicles to replace their current human-driven fleet as quickly as possible.

Similarly, 47% of long-haul trucking fees are paid to the drivers. That means the first company to introduce autonomous trucks will have a two-to-one price advantage over its competitors. That would allow market domination if left unchallenged. The net result will be a race against time for the entire industry to switch over to autonomous trucks. This transition will happen fast!

Going back to Uber, if 75% of the fares go to the driver, they could potentially reduce fares by 50% or more (allowing some money to cover the amortized cost of the vehicles themselves). Then, since electricity is 90% cheaper than gas on a per-mile basis, they could reduce the current pricing structure by 95%. The result is that autonomous electric transport might cost just 5% of current fares on a per-mile basis.

The average cost for Uber or Lyft rides in America is about $2 per mile. Tesla's CEO estimated that their robotaxi service will offer rides at about 18¢ per mile, or about 91% less than current rates. That's not 95%, but Tesla probably won't be the cheapest either.

At those rates, it will make zero sense for city residents to purchase their own vehicles unless they're driving enthusiasts or want to use their new autonomous vehicles to earn an income in the newly-transformed TaaS (Transport as a Service) market. There's one more variable to consider.

Today, the average vehicle is parked over 90% of the time. Some estimates suggest that usage hovers around 6%. The new TaaS vehicles will be driving the vast majority of the time. They will only park to be recharged, serviced, or due to low-demand conditions, so the utilization rate will be much higher. That means fewer cars will be required to provide the same level of mobility.

Having said that, the lower cost of transport will increase demand overall. If you can hail an autonomous car, outfitted with Wi-Fi connectivity, for 5% or 10% of today's Uber fares, you will be much more likely to do so. You could even go across long distances, not worrying about traffic or stress, because you'll be working away on your laptop. That means the overall miles traveled will rise on a per capita basis, meaning more traffic.

The analysis is fascinating. Since cars will be parked less, we'll need fewer parking lots, mainly in city centers. Parking structures account for more than 30% of land usage in some city centers. The parking structures outside the city centers may remain in place, but the street parking and extensive parking infrastructure in downtown areas will soon be a thing of the past.

That will allow countless premium real estate plots, currently occupied by parking lots, to be redeveloped into residential, commercial, or mixed-use structures. At the same time, the lower fares will result in more miles traveled, resulting in more traffic. So less parking, but more traffic.

Commercial TaaS Minibuses

It's also likely that large companies such as Starbucks might introduce autonomous minibuses that offer transport for free. At 5% of current Uber rates on a per-mile basis, and with six or more passengers in each minibus, the revenue potential of captive audiences in moving minibuses outfitted with small Starbucks kiosks will be more profitable than current advertising campaigns.

If the business model succeeds, there will likely be yoga buses, meditation buses, gaming buses, and educational buses as well. In this scenario, transport would be free for anyone willing to ride a corporate minibus. One might imagine a number of companies collaborating through a shared TaaS mobile app, allowing the public to hail a ride in whatever commercial minibus they wish.

Of course, social distancing guidelines will need to be considered too. I'm simply trying to give you a picture of what the world might look like in a few more years. It's possible that post-pandemic fear will subside in three or four years, so the public might be ready for the commercial minibus concept by the time the business model becomes viable.

Predicting Deployment

If you would like to have an idea when these technologies might be rolled out, it's useful to segment the market by the number of obstacles that vehicles encounter in different situations. Obviously, the environment with the most obstacles is dense inner-city streets. Imagine the obstacles and unexpected hazards on Manhattan's streets during rush hour, especially during a winter snow-storm. Due to these complexities, it's likely that this driving environment will be the last to be approved by regulators.

Suburban streets have fewer obstacles, and we already have a few pilot programs taking place in limited campuses and restricted neighborhoods. Level 4 autonomy is already approved in some parking structures in Germany, and there are many other pilot programs taking place around the world. Freeways have even fewer obstacles. For this reason, hub-to-hub long-haul autonomous trucking will probably be approved before autonomous driving on inner-city streets or in restricted campuses or urban neighborhoods.

Human drivers will still be required to drive the "last mile" into city streets. But even with that requirement, drivers will not necessarily be required to sit inside the trucks themselves. Instead, they might be sitting in business parks on the other side of the country, connected to the trucks' onboard cameras and controls like an expensive gaming station. These driving cubicles would be outfitted with steering wheels and acceleration and brake pedals, and allow remote drivers to operate autonomous trucks the same way Middle East drones are controlled by military personnel in Houston.

Finally, there remain certain environments that have even fewer obstacles than freeways, and those include agricultural land and mining operations. Autonomous driving has already been approved in those environments. The combines operating on corn fields in Iowa and Kansas are, in some cases, already driven autonomously. Farmers can map their land to the square inch and let the technology optimize the driving path. The same is true in large mines.

Understanding obstacle-based segments makes it easier to envision the timeline for Level 5 autonomous driving in city streets. Agriculture and mining operations were approved first. We can expect hub-to-hub long-haul trucking to be approved next, more Level 4 autonomy in restricted neighborhoods after that, and full Level 5 autonomy on congested city streets last.

I believe Level 5 autonomy will be approved in one state or another by 2023. The combination of inexpensive electric vehicles and Level 5 autonomy will bring a myriad of vehicle configurations to the market, ranging from small single-occupancy options to the commercial minibuses described earlier, and even large autonomous semi-trucks.

In a country like such as the USA, where the 50 states compete with each other for businesses and jobs, we can expect one state to lead the pack when it comes to autonomous driving regulations. I'm not sure which one yet, but it's guaranteed to happen somewhere first. Once initial approvals are in place, other states will feel the pressure to follow suit, and the transport revolution will shift into high gear.

The creative juices are already flowing. Scania, a Sweden-based company, has developed a modular truck that boasts a drivetrain substructure and different modular top configurations to serve different purposes. The same drivetrain substructure could propel a public transportation bus in the mornings and afternoons, a cargo truck during the day, and a garbage truck at night, allowing for the most efficient possible use of the drivetrain.

Job Losses and Retraining

Whether corporate minibuses succeed or fail, and regardless of the final order of regulatory approvals, autonomous transport will displace over 750,000 Uber drivers in the USA (2017 estimate). There are huge implications of these technologies on today's job markets. There are more than 3.5 million truck drivers in the USA and 8.7 million people directly or indirectly employed by that industry.

Earlier, we noted that there are more than 3.4 million retail cashiers at risk of losing their jobs as a result of self-checkout kiosks. Add another 8.7 million people employed in the trucking industry, and 750,000 ride-sharing drivers, and you end up with almost 13 million jobs at risk of being displaced by automation, and that's just in two industries (retail cashiers and professional drivers). That represents about 7.7% of the nation's workforce.

All of the trends discussed in this book have pros and cons. It's very rare indeed for something purely positive to emerge without a corresponding downside. The change is always bad for somebody. The same is true for automation, and the coming changes in our employment markets will drive the necessity for lifelong learning. People will need relevant skills to be employed in tomorrow's economy.

Some suggest that it's unreasonable to retrain a laid-off truck driver as a cloud engineer, and they are quite right. Although one or two success stories may appear, the vast majority of laid-off truck drivers will eventually secure new jobs that are somehow related to their previous jobs.

Imagine that the economy consists of 100,000 different jobs, and further assume that the bottom 100 or 200 get wiped out by automation. During the same time period, there will likely be 100 or 200 new jobs created at the very top of the list. Very few people, if any, from the bottom group of jobs will end up in the top group. Instead, all participants in the job market will probably move up a rung or two.

Back in the 1980s, there was concern that bank tellers would all lose their jobs as a result of the automated teller machines (ATMs) being introduced by banks. The interesting thing is that the total number of tellers didn't drop at all. In fact, it continued to rise over time, albeit at a much slower rate. Why?

ATMs allowed each bank branch to employ fewer tellers, and that reduced the break-even point of opening new branches. Before ATMs, banks only had branches in downtown centers. After ATMs started processing basic withdrawals and deposits, banks were able to open more branches in neighborhoods across the city. Each branch had fewer tellers than previous branches, but there were many more branches than before.

The tellers who remained were trained to do more complex and sophisticated tasks than previous bank tellers. They were able to do foreign currency conversions, cross-sell mortgage loan products, or discuss retirement account options. The result was that bank teller jobs became more sophisticated.

The same was not true for travel agents. As online platforms for booking flights, hotels, and rental cars improved, the number of travel agents steadily declined.

When considering automation options within your own business, ask yourself if the job losses will (1) result in lower break-even points, allowing for an expansion strategy, or (2) simply displace jobs permanently. Wherever possible, look for opportunities to lower your cost basis and expand your footprint within your marketplace.

Finally, some people are convinced that we'll lose over 40% of our jobs to automation, and the economy will collapse as a result. A few years back, a study from Oxford University suggested that 47% of American jobs were inherently repetitive and, therefore, at risk of being displaced by technology. As brutal as that figure sounds, the percentage was even higher for other countries such as China (77%) and India (69%).

History tells a different story. The countries that have adopted technology quickly have also, generally speaking, had the lowest levels of unemployment. Japan, South Korea, Germany, and the United States are all examples. Technology and employment are positively correlated.

Also, if massive job losses do actually materialize, entrepreneurs and business owners will see excess supply in the labor markets as a business opportunity. If there are people available who are looking for work, businesses will find a way to use that resource. It is admittedly possible that the new jobs will be lower-paying than the previous jobs, but new jobs will definitely be created.

The Future of Work

As an economy, we are trending towards higher and higher levels of service. One way to look at it is in the context of Maslow's Hierarchy of Needs. Two hundred years ago, most jobs filled the lowest Physiological needs category (food, water, shelter, clothing, etc.). Over time, productivity increased and new businesses catered to higher Safety needs (property, health, employment, etc.).

Social media platforms started to proliferate in the early 2000s. Facebook, Instagram, and YouTube fall into the third Love and Belonging category, and we already have many businesses catering to the fourth Self-Esteem level and also the fifth Self-Actualization level. Massage therapists, life and business coaches, meditation practitioners, and self-help gurus come to mind.

Many of the new businesses of the future will cater to these higher need levels. People in these fields sometimes talk about a great human awakening, but they've got the cart before the horse. This awakening is happening precisely because there are more practitioners in the field, and their collective advice is seeping into our cultural dialog. People are far more aware of meditation and mindfulness these days, and that will continue into the future.

Another model involves the (1) do it yourself, (2) done with you, and (3) done for you continuum. We are trending towards the 'done for you' model. People want results, and they're generally not confident in their own ability to execute the advice given. As a result, people are increasingly willing to pay extra to have someone come and essentially do the work for them. People want to buy results.

Businesses of the future will cater to highly evolved human needs and will simultaneously do most of the work for their customers. If you have the money, you can buy the reality you're looking for. As a business, the closer you can bring your customers towards their ultimate objectives, the better your products or services will sell. We'll see more of these types of options in the future.

Strategic Questions

As a business owner or executive decision-maker, you need to think about automation within your business. You need to look for ways to minimize human proximity and lower overall production costs. Here are a few questions to get you started.

- How can you increase automation in your business?

- How can you help your customers increase automation in their businesses?

- How can you better leverage the capabilities you have already paid for?

- Who on your team is best suited to data analytics?

- What are the repetitive tasks in your organization?

- Which repetitive tasks are likely to be automated first?

- How will the impending transportation revolution affect your business?

- What skills and personality traits do you need in your team?

PANDEMIC TREND #6: GOVERNMENT

Some people love big government. Others hate it. Some support global organizations such as the United Nations, the World Trade Organization, and the International Monetary Fund. Others want them defunded. This book will not favor one opinion over another. Rather, it will focus on the underlying trend, and that's towards more government programs and more government control. Whether you like government or not, there's no question that it has far more power than it did before this outbreak started.

We have already given up enormous personal freedoms since the pandemic was declared. Shelter-in-place orders, social distancing, and face masks have all become mandatory during the quarantine. Fear has spiked so much that people have begun "quarantine shaming" their neighbors and even calling the police when they see unauthorized gatherings.

This pandemic is turning into a massive power-grab by governments and globalists. Personally, I'm okay with that. I feel like the situation warrants a strong government response, but at the same time, there's no question that it's a power-grab. Pro-globalist pundits have lined up to tell us how important it is that we embrace these global organizations and trust their good intentions.

Here's the thing: For the most part, they've done a good job. Human metrics are getting better all the time. Infant mortality, life expectancy, death by disease, and even death by natural disaster have all gone down dramatically over the past decade or two. We've reduced poverty by more than half, and much of that work has been coordinated by global organizations.

This relates back to the biased and manipulative media industrial complex and people's negative perceptions when things are actually getting better. Media outlets have an incentive to publish negative news. When there's a car crash on the highway, everyone slows down to take a look. That doesn't happen when there's a beautiful field of flowers to look at. It only happens when there's something bad. If it bleeds, it leads. That's the media's mantra.

The same phenomenon happens with the state of the world and the steady improvement of human well-being metrics. Things have improved dramatically, but few realize it. Mostly due to the media, people believe the world is falling apart and that things have broadly gotten worse. It's not true. Watch some of the TED talks by Hans Rosling. He passed away in 2017 but did an amazing job in several appearances describing human progress. The world is getting better, not worse.

Anyway, this inaccurate negative perception makes people believe that these global organizations are doing a poor job. Because they think that the world is getting worse, they want to immediately blame the global organizations who were designed to improve things. And it's this hatred and suspicion of these global organizations that has fueled the many conspiracy theories being peddled these days.

Do government leaders and globalists want more power? Of course they do! Are there bad people in some of those positions who do shady things? Absolutely. But there are also a ton of well-intentioned people who work tirelessly to achieve the lofty goals these organizations were founded on. We have to keep a balanced view.

Political Perspectives

I have a somewhat unique perspective on politics. As just mentioned, human health metrics have been getting better each year. The world is improving. We've made incredible progress. So, as far as I'm concerned, the Republicans have done a great job. The Democrats have done a great job. The libertarians have done a great job. The globalists have done a great job. We're doing great, and it's gonna get even better!

Everyone wants to make the world better. Republicans, Democrats, libertarians, and globalists all want to improve our human experience on this planet. They just have different ways of doing it, that's all. They might have different strategies, and they might have different priorities, but they're all working toward the same goal. And, for the most part, they've succeeded.

I don't subscribe to the "world is falling apart" adage. It's not true. It's a manipulated narrative propagated by media outlets that profit from negative news. There's no question that we're in the middle of an unprecedented crisis. I acknowledge that 100%. But we'll get through this too, and I'm willing to bet the world will end up better as a result.

Don't get too worked up about petty politics. Have faith that people in power, generally speaking, have good intentions. Cast your ballot on Election Day and leave it at that. Worry about your micro-economy. That's far more important. Evaluate your industry and look for new opportunities. If we all spent a little less time watching the news, and a bit more time improving our businesses, we'd all be part of a thriving and exciting economy.

To be clear, I do have political preferences. I do think some strategies are better than others. I'm Canadian, of course, so I'm socially quite liberal, but I'm also quite conservative on fiscal issues. But whatever! I'm more worried about my own micro-economy. I worry about my career and my ability to earn a comfortable living.

Legislative Proposals

Anyway, the direction of progress in this world is generally good. I want to be clear on that point. I wish there were a way for everyone to see how much progress we've made. It's truly astounding. Having said that, however, are there also areas where we have to be careful? Yes, there are.

Within the halls of Congress, we've already had proposals for vaccine registries, allowing people to instantaneously know whether others have or have not had their vaccines. We've had proposals for the introduction of a digital dollar—a cryptocurrency equivalent to the US dollar. Neither of these proposals has found its way into legislation so far, but either could easily be adopted down the road.

Both of these proposals, and many others, would give government enormous additional powers while reducing our own individual freedoms. While I am strongly in favor of vaccines, a vaccine registry would force everybody to get their shots, regardless of their personal beliefs. A cryptocurrency dollar would leave behind a complete digital record of every single transaction made by every single person.

The biggest learning point from the Edward Snowden leaks in 2013 was that the National Security Agency (NSA) didn't need the contents of emails to identify suspicious actors. Instead, they simply needed to know who was communicating with whom, and how frequently they were communicating. With that information alone, they could map the population and identify those with nefarious intentions.

The same is true with cryptocurrency ledgers. It wouldn't show who made the purchase or exactly what they purchased, but the network of transactions would identify suspicious actors just as easily. Of course, there are some cryptocurrencies that provide higher levels of encryption and cloaking, but you can bet the government-sanctioned version would have plenty of back doors.

There are some who believe the famously unrevealed Bitcoin founder, Satoshi Nakamoto, was actually the CIA, knowing that the Bitcoin blockchain would leave digital breadcrumbs of every financial transaction. Also, the anonymous nature of cryptocurrencies would naturally attract those selling prohibited items (such as narcotics, weapons, etc.), and that would be of interest to the CIA too.

Still today, there are more than 1.5 million Bitcoins (worth over $12B at the time of this writing) that have been mined but never used. Furthermore, all of the earliest blocks were mined to a single payout address. It's difficult to believe that an individual could resist the urge to spend such vast wealth.

Anyway, both proposals (a vaccine registry and a crypto-currency version of the US dollar) would have benefits too. The trick would be to evaluate the benefits and risks in a balanced way. It's quite possible that the benefits outweigh the risks. The problem is that few people, especially those obsessed with conspiracy theories, would go through a proper evaluation before making their own conclusions.

Government Opportunities

As a business executive, you should be aware of both sides. There are people in your company who are strongly pro-government and pro-globalist. There are others who feel the opposite way, and the divide between these two groups is as stark as you can imagine. So regardless of your own opinions, try to be sensitive to the opposing views within your team.

The bottom line is that governments and central banks are pumping stimulus into our economy at unprecedented rates. They have huge budgets, and they're spending money.

- Can any of your products or services support their objectives?

Even if you hate government, it might represent a significant growth opportunity for you. They're spending money!

- What can you sell them?

Remember that there are many layers to government. The Federal government has some programs, but State governments have others. Municipal governments have programs of their own, including school districts, electric utilities, and police and fire departments. Once the quarantine is over, there will be enormous need for community outreach as governments try to keep their citizens solvent, engaged, and productive.

Think through the many programs being administered by one government department or another. Social security, food stamps (SNAP), Medicare and Medicaid, public and low-income housing, and school lunch programs are only a few that come to mind. Thousands of school districts and countless police and fire departments have needs too, and that doesn't even include the regular maintenance of city streets, water pipes, and electric grid infrastructure.

Ask yourself what you could do to support these government programs, and then reach out to let them know about your company and the products and services you offer. The trick is to find the right person within the department you're targeting. Focus your attention there. If you can send something to the right person, you might be surprised at the response you get.

A friend just sent out letters to repo managers at yacht dealers, manufacturers, and lenders. During the 2008 and 2009 financial crisis, many yachts were liquidated at rock bottom pricing, resulting in huge losses for these industry participants.

His letters reminded them of those losses and described the flawed incentive structure that led to the problem. He then described his own services as well as his independence from any single market participant. That independence allows him to seek the best deal for each individual boat. He has no incentive to close a bad deal. It takes more time, but the salvage value is dramatically higher.

He described his services in detail and did significant research to ensure his letters were sent to the right person within each organization. Although he started this campaign only last week, he's already heard back from about 20% of the letter recipients. That's an incredible response rate!

These yacht industry organizations aren't government departments, but the same model applies. Send thorough and thoughtful proposals to the right people, and then follow up with phone calls or emails. These are unprecedented times, and they need results. If you can help government get measurable results, they need to hear from you.

PANDEMIC TREND #7: EXPONENTIAL THINKING

We've been talking about exponential thinking for the past 10 years. Technology is evolving along an exponential curve, and that's challenging, because human beings are hardwired to think in linear terms. That's one of the primary reasons why the term "disruptive innovation" has become so popular. Yes, it existed before technology became so prevalent in business, but it's become far more relevant in today's technology-driven economy.

The nature of exponential growth is that the progression looks insignificant in the early days. It takes a while for the line to reach the proverbial hockey stick inflection point. Thereafter, it turns practically vertical. As a result, early technologies (such as the personal computer or the digital camera) seem like insignificant competitors at first, but then they start advancing so fast that you can no longer catch up.

Many smart and well-educated business executives have been caught off guard by exponential technologies. They may have known about them early on, but the acceleration of progress was insurmountable when they finally took action. As a business futurist, I spend my days researching exponential technologies, and I struggle with this too. I coach myself almost every day.

- What if this technology was 10 times as powerful as it is today?

- What if this technology was 100 times as powerful as it is today?

- What if this technology costs one tenth of what it costs today?

- What if this technology costs one hundredth of what it costs today?

The linear thinking instinct is very clear when watching a car, person, or animal moving across the horizon. It's very natural to observe the speed and then predict where it will be in five or 10 seconds. Every football quarterback does this when throwing the ball to receivers running downfield. But with exponential progression, it's much more difficult. After a slow start, the numbers accelerate quickly to the point where they're no longer comprehensible.

You've probably heard numerical comparisons before. If you took thirty steps in a linear sequence, you'd be about 75 feet down the road, assuming an average step of 2.5 feet. But if you took thirty steps in an exponential sequence where each step was double the previous step, you would've walked around the world nine times!

If you put one grain of rice in the first square of a checkers board, and then doubled it in each subsequent square, you'd end up exhausting the world's production of rice before reaching the last square.

We've already discussed this exponential progression with respect to data storage. The cost of storing one terabyte of data was $17,000 back in the year 2000, and it's dropped to just $3 in 2020. Likewise, the cost of PV solar panels has dropped by well over 99% since the 1970s. These are exponential progressions.

Well, for the first time, the general population truly understands exponential curves. We're living through it, day by day. We see the numbers of COVID-19 cases in our respective countries. I remember when the US had 75,000 cases, and then it doubled to 150,000 less than a week later. A few more days passed, and we had 300,000 cases, and then 600,000 cases.

People all around the world are digesting these daily increases. It's scary and sobering and shocking, but it also educates the public about this powerful phenomenon. Exponential growth is an incredible thing to witness, and it has relevance in many areas of our lives.

As already mentioned, exponential growth drives the technology industry. It affects the reality that a given set of performance metrics (data processing in desktops, laptops, or smartphones, for example) gets cheaper each year. It affects the reality that these same products are more powerful each year, allowing for more sophisticated software capabilities. It affects the reality that video games feature more detailed animation each year, and it affects emerging virtual reality capabilities as well.

Exponential growth also affects our investments through the much-discussed compound interest effect. Albert Einstein famously said that "the most powerful force in the universe is compound interest." If your investments achieved the same stable interest rate, year after year, with all paid interest reinvested, the most significant returns would come right at the end when the interest rate is applied to the largest capital base.

A $10,000 investment earning 7% interest would be generating over $9,000 *per year* after 40 years of compounded returns. That's more than 90% of the original investment, earned annually, and growing even more thereafter.

Exponential growth even affects climate change. Increasing per-capita energy consumption by an increasing population results in accelerating annual CO_2 emissions. The melting of the polar ice cap changes the surface color of those regions from white (snow) to dark blue (water), increasing the amount of sun's energy being absorbed and, as a result, accelerating the heating effect.

As oceans warm, not only do they grow in size (because warmer water takes up more space than colder water, resulting in rising sea levels), but warmer water also causes more frequent and severe storm systems. It's an exponential progression. They all have a compounding effect.

Deploying Technology

As a business executive, you need to think in exponential terms. Regardless of the industry you're in, technology will continue to play an increasing role in your business model, and technology evolves along an exponential curve.

Think about the most recent form of technology you deployed in your business.

- What if it was 10 times as powerful as it is today?

- What if it cost one tenth of what you paid for it?

- How many of your competitors would be using the same technology if it was available at that lower price?

If any given level of technology comes down in price over time, you need to think about the most cost-effective time to invest in it. The well-known "first mover advantage" implies that the first to deploy benefits the most. That can certainly be true, but the "second mover advantage" allows businesses to obtain the same benefits at a lower cost.

- When's the right time to pull the trigger?

Make a list of the biggest players in your industry, and then sort that list by their gross profit. If they are publicly traded companies, this information is easy to find. If they're private companies, it's more difficult, but do the best you can.

Keep in mind that gross profit is different from gross margin. Gross margin is the percentage of margin you have in each product or service, after deducting the cost of goods sold (COGS). Gross profit is the aggregate amount of gross margin across all sales.

There are two different ways to achieve gross profit. You can sell a few products at a high margin, or you can sell many products at a low margin. Ideally, you could have both: sell many products at a high margin. That's the best-case scenario, but it's difficult to achieve in today's competitive marketplace. The best example is probably Apple's iPhone. It's a high-margin product, and they sell a ton of them! The same is true for luxury brands, but all of these brands require extensive marketing campaigns to support their elite brand image.

Most companies fall into one of the two initial categories. China, for example, is well known for seeking volume above all else. They want to sell a ton of products, and they're willing to take lower margins to secure those sales. Even at low margins, high-volume sales still end up generating significant gross profit levels. Other companies sell fewer items but have higher margins, so they obtain their gross profit that way. Sort your competitors by their total gross profit.

New technologies generally deploy in the same order. The companies with the highest gross profit can afford to develop and deploy new technologies more quickly. Companies with lower gross profit deploy later, and the companies at the bottom of the list deploy last.

Determine where your business is on that list. This will provide some guidance on your investment strategy, relative to your competition. It will give you an idea as to when you need to pull the trigger.

When it comes to technology, the first companies to deploy need to develop the capability themselves. As the first to pursue it, by definition, the capability doesn't exist yet. That means they have to pay for the development phase and the inevitable trial and error process that takes place. That's expensive.

After the capability is fully developed, deployed, and well understood, the enterprise software companies (including ERP and CRM companies) start incorporating the new capability in their software packages. We discussed this in the Analytics chapter.

This was evident when "big data" technologies emerged in 2011 and 2012. The first companies to deploy that scale of data processing paid huge sums to develop the capability. Traditional relational databases weren't able to process that much data, so new "parallel processing" capabilities (including Hadoop and Spark, et al.) needed to be developed first. It was expensive.

I saw a study once that sent questionnaires to enterprise IT professionals within Fortune 500 companies. This was back in 2013, I believe, and the responses suggested that the average ROI from big data technologies was *negative* 45%! These large companies were actually *losing* money on their early investments. They were looking for gold in all that data but only finding sand.

It took time for profitable use cases to emerge. As mentioned in the Analytics section, predictive maintenance was an early winner in the big data space, and a few others showed promise as well. The first companies to dig into those technologies paid huge sums in the development phase. But eventually, those same capabilities were incorporated in standard ERP and CRM platforms. At that point, the incremental cost of deployment had dropped dramatically.

If you're using enterprise software-as-a-service (SaaS) platforms in your business, incorporate this knowledge in your IT investment strategy. The capabilities you're looking for might come to you all on their own! Of course, you may still need to develop some custom applications, but the underlying capability will be cheaper if you can wait for your software platforms to provide it.

The point of this discussion is to streamline your thinking and give you a structured way to consider future investments. Remember, for the foreseeable future, the #1 priority is to preserve your liquidity. It might make sense to wait a year to leverage new capabilities at a lower cost.

Adoption "S" Curves

New technology *adoption* follows an exponential curve too, but that curve flattens out when approaching market saturation. You can't go beyond 100% saturation, so the resulting adoption curve is often referred to as an "S" curve. It starts out slow, then accelerates dramatically (and exponentially) through the 16% critical mass point and all the way up to about 80% adoption, and then slows down considerably as market saturation is reached.

Tony Seba, keynote speaker and author of "Clean Disruption of Energy and Transportation" (2014, Tony Seba, Beta edition) often shows two photographs of 5th Avenue in New York City. The first was taken in 1900, and it shows dozens of horse-drawn carriages. If you look closely, you can see one single automobile in the photo. The second was taken in 1913, and it shows the dozens of automobiles on the same street. If you look closely, you can see one single horse in the photo. The automobile disruption took just 13 years to reach broad market adoption.

In "The Tipping Point" (2002, Back Bay Books), Malcolm Gladwell highlights the importance of reaching 16% market penetration, and how awareness and adoption accelerated dramatically after that. He was referring to the first half of the "S" curve. Keep these "S" curves in mind as you evaluate new innovations in your industry. If one is approaching that magical 16% mark, adoption could accelerate quickly thereafter.

Strategic Questions

These realities should shape your thinking. This is what strategy is all about. These are models to anticipate future events. You can lead your company strategically with these models in mind.

- How can you incorporate exponential thinking into your business?

- What innovations should you consider investing in?

- Where do you fall on the gross profit continuum within your industry?

- Can you help your customers navigate exponential innovations in their own industries?

The public's new understanding of exponential growth might also affect your product or service development process as well as your marketing strategy. If the public now finally understands exponential growth, it might make sense to incorporate that into your messaging.

- How can you incorporate exponential thinking into your marketing?
- Is there a way to exploit public understanding of exponential growth?

PANDEMIC TREND #8: DECENTRALIZATION

One prevailing trend encompasses most of the others: decentralization. There are a few exceptions, and we'll discuss those, but decentralization seems to underpin most of the other trends. I wrote about this extensively in my last book, "Anarchy, Inc.: Profiting in a Decentralized World with Artificial Intelligence and Blockchain" (2018, Authority Publishing). You're welcome to purchase that book (available on Amazon), but you should know that the content overlaps this chapter to some extent.

Consider a few examples. We used to have about a dozen large media outlets (centralized). Today, we have millions to choose from (decentralized). Power used to be exclusively generated by massive hydroelectric dams and coal, natural gas, and nuclear power plants (centralized). Today, we increasingly have solar panels on the roofs of millions of homes around the world (decentralized). Our monetary system has thus far been managed by central banks (centralized). Over the last 10 years, we've seen cryptocurrencies such as Bitcoin emerge with blockchain architecture (decentralized).

Echo Chambers

The COVID-19 pandemic will accelerate this trend toward economic, social, and political decentralization. Social distancing and working from home are reducing human proximity, and people will be left fearful even after a vaccine has been developed. People are increasingly shopping and interacting online, and data-driven market segmentation by advertisers is resulting in finely tuned echo chambers to satisfy every possible opinion.

Political echo chambers have shown their colors throughout this crisis. Democrats started quarantines earlier than Republicans. After enforcement, Republicans wanted to open up faster than Democrats. Democrats want more government support. Republicans want to open the economy and get back to work. Democrats believe the most extreme interpretations of the data, and many Republicans believe it's all a big lie.

There's some intuitive logic behind these differences. Political preferences in the United States have a lot more to do with population density than anything else. Densely-populated urban areas have more crime, poverty, and income inequality, so the need for social services is more apparent to residents. Meanwhile, rural areas have less of all thee, and also have stronger religious affiliations, all of which feed directly into more conservative political views.

Within each political camp, there are many subgroups. At the same time, of course, there are exceptions to every generalization. No matter what your personal opinions are, even before this pandemic hit, there were online influencers and media outlets that catered to your particular combination of opinions.

Two decades ago, we had about a dozen large media outlets. Today, we have literally millions of options. Blogs, social media influencers, podcasts, traditional media outlets, and TV channels each cater to one opinion or another, and each one accuses the others of "fake news" and bias. That's a decentralized marketplace. It's a form of anarchy.

My "Anarchy, Inc." book is about that phenomenon specifically. When you have huge numbers of market participants, and nobody trusts one central authority, that's a form of anarchy. It doesn't mean you have violence on the streets. It doesn't mean you necessarily have street gangs and neighborhood gun battles. Anarchy simply means the population rejects a set hierarchy and the community operates without a central governing authority.

From a societal perspective, we're not at that stage yet, but we see glimpses in that direction, and there's reason to believe the trend will continue. Our media environment is already in anarchy. Politics is close behind. Even education and e-commerce are drifting in that direction.

Societies will become more fragmented, multiculturalism will recede, and social groups will become more tribal. We will all find and follow our own experts, influencers, mentors, and gurus.

Multiple Realities

The net result is a world with multiple realities, literally, and multiple versions of the "truth." Think about this from a supply-and-demand perspective. When you have limited information, you take whatever is available. Henry Ford famously said, "You can have whatever color you want as long as it's black." Limited supply means limited options. But when you have surplus information, you can pick whatever you like and ignore the rest.

We have surplus information today. Three hundred hours of video content are uploaded to YouTube every single minute. There's no way for any one person to consume all of the available content. On the contrary, you can consume only a minuscule percentage. Just like our conscious awareness, discussed in the Automation chapter (and also in my TEDx Talk), you're only aware of a tiny slice of the content being generated.

Surplus information means that you have to pick the content you consume and, more importantly, you have to intentionally reject the content you don't want. The content is coming at you so fast, you have to consciously reject the stories you're not interested in.

Not surprisingly, most people select the stories they already agree with or, at a minimum, the stories that are consistent with their view of the world. That creates echo chambers where we see only those views we already agree with, making it almost impossible to empathize with people who think differently than we do.

There is always ample evidence to support our opinions, regardless how crazy or outlandish they might be. That's why conspiracy theories have proliferated so much in recent years. If you search on Google for conspiracies about 9/11, the military industrial complex, the oil industry, the eugenics movement, climate change "alarmists," population control, chemtrails, vaccines, the Bretton Woods conference, Bohemian Grove, Denver airport, Malaysian Airlines flight MH370, Sandy Hook, or "false flag" events attributed to Iran or the Bashar al-Assad regime in Syria, you'll find overwhelming affirming "evidence" in each case.

The result is multiple realities and multiple versions of the truth. Long before the novel coronavirus was discovered in China, we already lived in a post-truth world. Donald Trump is famous for bending facts to fit his narrative. "Alternative facts" have become ubiquitous.

Is China lying about their COVID-19 data? Probably, but it's impossible to prove one way or the other. Are globalists leveraging this crisis to fund their favorite program proposals? Probably, but we'll never know for sure. Is George Soros happy about this situation? What about Bill Gates? So many "sources" are sowing seeds of doubt that it's difficult to trust anyone. That's all part of anarchy, and it's all fueling the trend toward decentralization.

Speak Your Truth

With multiple versions of the truth, your business needs to pick the version you subscribe to, then market to those who identify with those same beliefs, and ignore everybody else. If you try to appeal to too many people, your message becomes diluted, and its appeal diminishes. The key is to stake your claim boldly and stick to it regardless of the criticism you receive from outside your tribe.

This is Trump's playbook. He speaks to his base, and he doesn't care what anyone else thinks. His constant exaggerations, online trolling, and inappropriate pronouncements drive establishment intellectuals crazy, but he doesn't care. He's chosen his version of the truth, and he's sticking with it. Meanwhile, his base can't get enough of his perceived candor and authenticity. The loyalty of his base is unmatched across the political spectrum.

Whether you love Donald Trump or hate him, you have to give him credit. He is a ratings king and has found a way to connect with supporters in a way few politicians can replicate. That makes him a model worth following, even if you hate his politics. Pick your reality and stick with it. Speak defiantly against your detractors and double down when challenged. Ignore your critics and stand firm in your truth.

Look at all the influencers making their rounds on Twitter, Instagram, Twitch, and Tik-Tok. They aren't soft apologetic personalities. No, they speak their truth confidently and ignore the haters. They've chosen their stance and rarely concede anything to their critics.

Make a list of the influencers you identify with most, and analyze their communication styles. Your marketing and branding needs to lean in their direction. This is a time for bold leadership. Your business needs to be defiant with its values and mission.

Passion sells. This has always been true. The only thing that's new today is the sheer number of corporate brands and influencers competing for our attention. But as long as societies have existed, passionate politicians have received more votes, passionate preachers accumulated more followers, passionate entertainers sold more albums, and passionate businesses made more sales.

Donald Trump is adored for his passionate rejection of establishment politics. Pastor Jentezen Franklin is adored for his passionate interpretation of the Bible. The Artist Formerly Known as Prince was adored for his passionate songs and performances, and Apple is adored for its passionate devotion to the rebels and misfits.

A friend called me in 2008 to ask my opinion of his support for California Proposition 8 which eliminated rights of same-sex couples to marry. He asked if I thought it would hurt him to include his stance on his LinkedIn profile. I said no, emphatically. His views are his views, whether I agree with them or not. Meanwhile, he's very active in his church, so his circle of influence is probably open to his stance anyway.

The bottom line is that his "fans" will like him more, not less, if he defends his views publicly. He gains respect from his community. He assumes a leadership role on the issue, as does anyone willing to express their views publicly and defiantly. As for the people who feel differently, they just don't matter. In fact, their outrage often magnifies exposure.

Jordan Peterson is a perfect example of this. He's a Canadian author, clinical psychologist, and scholar who gained enormous prominence when he expressed his views on gender pronoun usage and identity politics. His views ran counter to mainstream liberal dogma, and a variety of media outlets interviewed him, stoking outrage in search of ratings. Those interviews, all designed to challenge his beliefs, ended up propelling him to stardom within his genre.

He went on to sell millions of copies of his book "12 Rules for Life: An Antidote to Chaos" (2019, Penquin) and embarked on a global speaking tour, selling out enormous theaters at $75 per ticket or more. The more defiant his rhetoric became, the more exposure he received. No press is bad press.

The essence of decentralization is that we're identifying with narrower ideologies and smaller groups. We agree with some Democratic priorities but disagree with others. We agree with some Republican priorities but disagree with others. An increasing percentage of voters self-identify as Independents. People are no longer identifying with large broad classifications. They're becoming more individual. Everyone has a unique combination of viewpoints.

Obviously, I'm not suggesting you declare wildly unpopular views publicly and hope for amazing results. You need to evaluate your marketplace and be discerning with the values you adopt. Calculations need to be made to ensure your targeting captures enough eyeballs to keep your business profitable and growing. My point is that passion and a touch of defiance go a long way when building loyalty within your marketplace.

As a business owner or executive decision-maker, now more than ever, choose your version of reality and communicate it passionately to your audience. They want to see your purpose. They want to know your cause.

Social Media Effects

Social media platforms exacerbate social polarization. We all have an instinct to post the best photos of our best activities to our social media profiles. The result is an image of our lives that does not reflect reality. The vast majority of social media profiles are collages of the best of the best, not the average. When we see these posts and compare them with our own lives, it's difficult not to feel inadequate by comparison.

This is happening across our entire population, but it's most damaging for teenagers. Competition during those years is fierce, and teenagers can be incredibly cruel to one another. The result is higher levels of anxiety and depression within our youth. Suicide used to be restricted mostly to boys and men, but recent years have seen a dramatic increase in female incidences.

For some businesses, this represents another opportunity.

- Can your products or services help people struggling with mental illness?

- Can your business help mitigate the destructive aspects of social media?

Social media has many benefits. As a population, we're more connected than ever. But it's also destroying the social fabric of our culture. Constant competition with wildly unrealistic depictions of our lives is breeding mental illness for millions.

I have noticed this in my own life. As a keynote speaker, I travel to conferences regularly, and many of them take place in exotic destinations. I often post photos of the places I visit, and my online connections inevitably believe that I have a perfect life with endless exciting adventures. There are many advantages to my career, and I am indeed grateful, but my life is far from perfect.

On Valentine's Day in 2015, I wasn't in a romantic relationship and decided to attend an annual public pillow fight in downtown San Francisco. Hundreds of people show up each year, armed with their own pillows, and fight it out in a public plaza at the intersection of Market Street and Embarcadero. I had no date, and I had no pillows. I just sat there and watched the spectacle, taking photos.

I posted a few of those photos on Facebook that evening, and a bunch of my friends liked the post, many expressing jealousy of the fun adventure I had been part of. They thought it was a happy, joyous evening for me. The truth was that I was miserable, and the spectacle of people pounding each other with pillows only made it worse.

Very few of those people came by themselves. They were there with friends or relationship partners. Love was in the air. I had none of that. I was there by myself, and didn't even participate. The event just reminded me of what I did *not* have in my own life!

We've probably all had similar experiences. Social media allows us to be connected to more people than ever before, but it's also driving us further apart. That's another reason for the echo chambers we cocoon ourselves in. We don't feel comfortable when we're surrounded by competitive people who judge us by unrealistic criteria. We'd rather engage with people who seem similar to ourselves.

Although we're more connected than ever, social media also contributes to the trend towards decentralization and isolation. As individuals, we need to remind ourselves not to interpret social media posts as reality. They're not. And as parents, we need to coach our children to do the same. Social media posts are not an accurate reflection of people's lives. They are choreographed moments with digital filters to make us look better than we do in real life.

The world is changing much faster than our biology can adapt. Human instincts evolve over tens of thousands of years, but we're being forced to navigate vastly different incentive structures than we had just 10 years ago. As human beings, we have a need for belonging and acceptance. We need validation from our peers, but social media quite often gives us the opposite.

Workforce Decentralization

Decentralization overlaps Self-Sufficiency (Trend #1), because they both advocate off-grid living and libertarian political views. They both appeal to populists and nationalists. At the extreme, decentralization implies completely independent and off-grid living.

Decentralization also overlaps Virtualization (Trend #4). With the prospect of working from home on an upswing, the need for local talent within your organization diminishes. Particularly for office and management jobs, traditional proximity limitations disappear. If you can find the right talent across the country or across the world, you can hire that person as easily as you can hire someone down the street. In fact, in some cases, it might be easier, and cost less.

The Results Only Work Environment (ROWE) is a recent innovation in human resources strategy that compensates employees based on results only. Nobody tracks the number of hours worked or when those hours were worked. Employees are welcome to get their work done in any fashion they like, as long as it meets the deadline and satisfies the expectations set out by management. This approach to hiring will accelerate in the future.

Take some time to think about the implications for your own organization.

- Where is your executive team located?

- How do they meet and interact with each other?

- How would a remote contributor affect the rest of the team?

- What if *all* team members were remote?

As long as team members can communicate with each other and get their work done, proximity is no longer essential.

The other consideration is that the cost of living varies dramatically in different parts of the world. It costs less to hire a university-educated professional in India or the Philippines than it does to hire the same qualifications in America. It's never advisable to look at compensation requirements alone, but it's certainly possible to find well-qualified candidates who cost a lot less.

The idea of decentralized management teams has many advantages. Businesses are increasingly global, and it's useful to have someone in a particular locale when expanding into that market. You benefit from having different perspectives when making strategic decisions. The company also becomes more aware of and responsive to local events such as hurricanes, typhoons, cyclones, droughts, fires, or earthquakes.

Information Technology Infrastructure

Decentralization affects resource allocation. The emergence of cloud computing during the past 15 years, driven by companies such as Amazon Web Services (AWS) and Microsoft's Azure platform, resulted in enormous data centers being constructed around the world. Over the past five years, we've seen a trend towards hybrid cloud architecture and edge computing.

Hybrid cloud is an environment that includes on-premise (or even on-device), private cloud, and public cloud components. Edge computing simply refers to the shift from centralized data processing (in huge public cloud data centers) to processing infrastructure that's closer to the actual customer. In many cases, edge devices may even replace the need for the private cloud layer.

This cloud architecture introduces new complexities for software developers, but it also reduces latency (because data processing is taking place "on the edge") and diversifies the operational risk over a broader network of IT facilities. If something horrible takes place in one facility, redundancies within the network mitigate downside risk, making the system more resilient.

If you take the edge computing trend to the extreme, one might imagine ubiquitous processing power available through any electrical outlet or Wi-Fi network.

Processing power would be completely commoditized in that scenario, leaving software as the only asset differentiating one participant from another. Whether the trend extends to that extreme or not, the importance of software is definitely increasing.

SD-WAN is a good example. It's an acronym that stands for software-defined wide area network. Data routing and cybersecurity protections used to involve actual hardware, but SD-WAN decouples the functionality from the hardware and manages everything with software alone. That results in fewer "hard" bottlenecks and better optimization possibilities. IT infrastructure is increasingly being managed by software.

AWS currently operates more than 30% of the cloud, and Microsoft Azure is gaining ground fast. Both built enormous data centers when cloud computing first gained traction, but they're both now building smaller edge computing infrastructure closer to city centers. Microsoft's Project Natick, for example, involves underwater data centers that can be maintained directly offshore from large urban centers. So even with these market-leading providers, we see the trend towards more decentralized offerings.

Blockchain Protocol

Blockchain represents another push towards decentralized systems. The primary benefit of blockchain protocol is its decentralized architecture and the fact that it is controlled by no single entity. Blockchain operates on a consensus mechanism that allows non-trusting parties to transact commerce with each other without worrying about cheating or manipulation of transaction data.

If you're unfamiliar with blockchain protocol, imagine an Excel spreadsheet with a list of transactions. But instead of that Excel spreadsheet existing on just one computer, it's actually stored on hundreds or even thousands of different servers simultaneously. Each server is referred to as a "node" on the network. Because of this network of nodes, blockchain can be thought of as a distributed ledger.

Every time a new "block" of transactions (think of a new Excel spreadsheet) is added to the "chain" of previous blocks (hence, the term blockchain), 51% of the nodes have to agree that they have the latest and most accurate version. Also, each new block has a summary of the previous block (called a "hash") embedded inside. Between these two characteristics, the consensus mechanism and embedded hashes, blockchain ledgers are extremely difficult to hack.

For a hack to be successful, it would need to successfully manipulate 51% of the nodes in exactly the same way and at the exact same time. Otherwise, the attempted hack would automatically be detected and averted.

Also, once something is on the blockchain, it's impossible to change it later, because you would have to change every subsequent block as well (because the hashes on subsequent blocks would change when data is manipulated), and those changes would have to be made on 51% of the nodes simultaneously. It's almost impossible to hack a blockchain.

The Bitcoin blockchain has never been successfully hacked. Various exchanges and wallets have definitely been hacked (including Mt. Gox in 2011, BitFloor in

2012, Poloniex in 2014, Bitstamp in 2015, Bitfinex in 2016, the DAO in 2016, and many others), but nobody has ever hacked the actual Bitcoin blockchain. And believe me—many have tried!

Blockchain automates trust. It's a software architecture that's secure by design, and no one entity controls it. That's why it's so powerful. It allows businesses to transact commerce with other businesses or people that they don't necessarily trust, and that's a central characteristic of our economy.

When blockchain first debuted in 2009, and again when Bitcoin had its first major price spike in 2013, many people were anticipating that the technology would soon replace banks, insurance companies, and regulatory authorities. Even democratic voting could be facilitated through a blockchain platform.

That may indeed happen one day, but it'll take time. Many challenges remain, including latency and interoperability issues, so these top-level applications have yet to materialize.

Another problem with blockchain systems is that they remain too complex for the average person to interact with. For any technology to gain broad market adoption, it must be easy to use. An intuitive user interface must be developed. Apple is famous for making the personal computer easy to use. They did the same thing for MP3 players and smartphones. Although many people are working on an effective user interface for cryptocurrencies, none has achieved the levels necessary to reach critical mass.

Blockchain Use Cases

Currently, leading blockchain use cases include (1) supply chain management, (2) digital identity, and (3) digital payments. There are others, of course, but these three applications have seen impressive development in recent years. In all three cases, the decentralized architecture is pivotal to the value proposition.

Consider a supply chain with manufacturers, distributors, and retailers, all transacting business with each other in order to provide products to consumers. If all of these businesses maintained their own nodes within a blockchain network, they could all add verification data as products travel through the supply chain, and they could also validate these various steps through the consensus mechanism. The net result would be complete transparency and traceability, all facilitated through a decentralized system.

Digital identity has similar benefits. Microsoft and Accenture collaborated to create ID2020 in 2017. It's a multi-stakeholder model for a user-managed, privacy-protected, and portable digital ID. Today, it includes an alliance of partner organizations that have a collective footprint in the billions as well as a shared commitment to ethical deployment. Again, the strength of this platform is its decentralized architecture.

Digital payments have not evolved much past the emergence of cryptocurrencies in general. They're definitely being traded a lot, offering unmatched volatility for traders and speculative investors, but they aren't commonly used to conduct regular commerce. Very few people are using Bitcoin to buy new boots or a cup of coffee.

Nevertheless, even the trading transactions are validated through the decentralized consensus mechanism.

The problem with decentralized solutions is that they reduce the power of all individual participants. No single entity controls a blockchain platform, so all existing participants lose some control when adopting a blockchain solution. Banks and insurance companies have enormous power and influence, and they'll fight to maintain that. Governments will too. It will be difficult for top-level applications to gain traction, because they'll be strongly resisted by established stakeholders.

If the credit-based monetary system collapses, as suggested earlier in this book, Bitcoin would be the primary winner, and the top-level applications of blockchain technology may finally start to arise. It all depends on the scale of the crisis within financial markets.

Establishment resistance will be fierce, but it is indeed possible if credit markets seize and/or people lose confidence in the banking system. Again, I'm not predicting that this will happen, but it certainly *could* happen if the financial crisis accelerates.

Anyway, blockchain is yet one more example of the trend towards decentralized systems. Cryptocurrencies represent a decentralized monetary system controlled by no single entity. It's the wet dream of every libertarian purist.

It would be similar to re-establishing the gold standard. Because the total number of Bitcoin is limited to 21 million, and with each additional Bitcoin being harder to mine than the last, it has similar characteristics to gold and would eliminate the inflationary effects of central banks printing money as they're doing today.

While money printing and quantitative easing haven't resulted in significant inflation within consumer markets, they have significantly inflated asset prices, particularly in real estate and financial assets like stock market equities. This directly benefits those who own assets, and it reduces the relative wealth of those who do not. In other words, it increases the division between rich and poor.

Many Bitcoin enthusiasts see that as a manipulation by central banks that unjustly punish the poor while rewarding the rich. Again, libertarian overtones creep in. Theoretically, Bitcoin would level the playing field and restore justice to the competitive pressures within free market capitalism, and there are some good reasons to believe it may eventually have its day in the sun.

Containing Decentralization

The interesting thing about this trend towards decentralization is that any efforts to contain it generally have the opposite effect. When governments have introduced restrictions on Bitcoin, for example, its price generally went up, not down.

A similar progression played out in Hawaii's energy markets. Hawaii has the highest adoption rates of solar power in America. Approximately 12% of homes in Hawaii have solar panels on their roofs. Initially, those with solar panels could mostly offset their normal electricity bills and, in some cases, even earn money by selling excess electricity back to the grid.

The problems started because the majority of electricity grid costs are not "variable" in nature. Instead, they are "fixed" expenses, meaning they don't vary as total output or demand varies. Fixed expenses are incurred regardless of how much is sold in the marketplace. The cost of maintaining electricity grid infrastructure is huge. Power plants, transformer stations, electric power poles, and wire maintenance all need to be paid for either way.

Since 12% of homeowners were largely avoiding electricity bills, the fixed expenses were being allocated over the remaining 88% of homes. Homeowners without solar panels claimed they were unfairly punished because their payments had to cover 100% of these fixed expenses. Homeowners with solar panels were benefiting from the grid but weren't paying for it.

The electric utility decided to charge a fixed fee to *all* customers, just to be connected to the grid. That fee was designed to level the playing field between homes with solar panels and those without. Of course, that was seen as unfair to those who made the significant investment to install solar panels. As a result, some of them purchased Tesla Powerwall units to balance peak generation periods (when the sun is shining) and peak usage periods, thereby allowing them to disconnect from the grid entirely.

The electric utility was in a catch-22. If they allocated fixed expenses only over paying customers, it was unfair to those *without* solar panels. If they charged a fixed fee to everyone, it was unfair for those *with* solar panels, and some would disconnect completely, making the problem even worse. The electric utility was screwed either way.

Many utility companies will face this quandary in the years ahead, as well as banks and insurance companies. Sooner or later, blockchain technology infrastructure will improve sufficiently to facilitate the switch from centralized institutions to decentralized alternatives. At that point, any attempts to slow the trend will actually do the opposite.

Centralized versus Decentralized

One of Indian Prime Minister Narendra Modi's greatest accomplishments is the introduction of the Aadhaar system, a biometric database that provides every Indian resident with a random 12-digit number used to administer social services. More than 99% of Indian adults have applied for and received their Aadhaar number. The application process is free of charge and includes a variety of demographic information as well as fingers prints, iris scans, and a facial photograph.

It's an impressive program, far more sophisticated than the American social security number. At the same time, however, the program is expensive to run and employs huge numbers of people to administer.

Meanwhile, ID2020 is a blockchain-based digital identity ledger, which has the potential to offer similar benefits at a fraction of the cost. Although plenty of money has been spent during the development phase, once fully deployed, the ledger should mostly run itself with limited maintenance costs.

The comparison of these two programs is fascinating. The Aadhaar program is limited by geography (only available in India) and costs a lot of money to operate.

ID2020 is not limited by any borders and costs far less to operate. On top of that, ID2020 isn't controlled by any single entity and is completely transparent to its users. The winner is clear.

I have no idea what the future holds for either of these two programs, but it is representative of countless contests in other fields. If you run this competition a thousand times, the blockchain model will win the majority of those contests. It's a more effective model and costs less to administer. Over a period of time, it's inevitable that blockchain solutions will emerge and successfully challenge existing institutions.

Open Source Software

The problem is that blockchain is essentially a public utility. Since it's controlled by no single entity, the opportunities for profit are limited. If you decide to build a blockchain, by definition, you need to collaborate with other market participants, including suppliers and customers and possibly even competitors. That's why many large players have resisted it so far.

Think about the open source software platform that acts as the foundation for the entire Internet: Linux. Open source software is developed under the General Public License (GPL) where the copyright holder grants users the right to change, upgrade, and distribute the source code. The result is software that is consistently improved by developers around the world, and it's free to use.

The question is: How can you make money from Linux? Thousands of companies have been formed around the Linux ecosystem. They compete with each other to make improvements to the platform for all to see, earning respect from developers and users alike. These companies then sell consulting contracts to develop custom applications and add-ons for large-scale users. In other words, the basic software is free, but companies sell custom upgrades and training.

Blockchain will evolve the same way. Sooner or later, in one industry after another, blockchain platforms will be built and deployed for a collaborative greater good, and the original developers will then make money by selling related and specialized services. At this stage, it's difficult to anticipate what those related services will be, but the business model exists already in the open source ecosystem.

Open source is another great example of decentralization. Linux is open source, but so are Apache, WordPress, Drupal, TensorFlow, and Kubernetes, among many others. The development of these "free" software packages is completely decentralized, but they each support thriving ecosystems of for-profit businesses. The foundations are public utilities, but the after-market customizations are for-profit options.

Centralized Power Play

This brings up another interesting paradox. While the trend toward decentralization is well underway, there are also technology infrastructure providers that are *gaining* enormous power, not losing it. Consider Google, Apple, Facebook, and Amazon, to name a few. They each provide platforms on which other businesses are built.

Millions of profitable businesses (including mine) spend huge sums with Google on advertising solutions. Apple has their App Store with millions of apps available, each with its own business model. Facebook hosts millions of groups and pages, and it sells tons of advertising too. Amazon is a retail platform with millions of products sold by millions of different vendors.

Amazon Web Services (AWS) is a cloud computing platform that hosts thousands of other businesses including LinkedIn, Facebook, Netflix, Twitch, the BBC, Baidu, and ESPN, among others. In many cases, there are literally platforms on top of other platforms. People have begun referring to today's technology environment as the "platform economy."

These technology infrastructure providers are becoming incredibly powerful. Google, Apple, Facebook, and Amazon are more powerful than many national governments, yet they're consolidating their power (centralizing) by providing the infrastructure for increasingly decentralized markets. In a sense, they are acting as the open source software foundation upon which thriving ecosystems are flourishing.

It's possible that even these technology behemoths may eventually be replaced by open source alternatives. In fact, over time, perhaps the entire economy will move to a more decentralized open source model.

Imagine an open source Uber without the company Uber. It would simply be a free platform connecting drivers with people who need a ride, but there would be nobody in the middle collecting 20% of the fees. Imagine an open source Airbnb without the company Airbnb. Imagine an open source PayPal without the company PayPal. That's what Bitcoin is! It's an open source peer-to-peer PayPal without the company PayPal.

This transition could take a long time, but it is indeed possible eventually. The entire economy will operate on decentralized platforms that offer public utility-type institutions, and businesses will provide products and services within those markets.

We're still in the early stages of these possible eventualities, but it's important for you to see how they're all connected under the same macro trend. Markets, networks, and human interactions will become more decentralized over time. Populations will become more tribal and less cohesive. Multiple versions of the "truth" will be held within the larger population, and the echo chambers that have already emerged will become even more pronounced.

At the same time, it's important to see that *some* market participants are bucking the trend. Large technology infrastructure providers are consolidating power. They appear to be contradicting the trend, but it remains possible that they too will be replaced eventually. Either way, it's insightful to watch these flourishing for-profit ecosystems evolve on top of different technology platforms.

Strategic Questions

As a business owner or executive decision-maker, you need to see the forces reshaping our societies. Decentralization is accelerating in many ways, and there may be opportunities you can capitalize on.

- Can you hire top-quality talent in non-local markets?

- Can you cultivate a decentralized management structure?

- Can you help organizations support the trend towards decentralization?

- Can you help people thrive in an increasingly decentralized world?

- What thriving ecosystems are emerging on top of technology platforms in your industry?

- Can you sell products or services within those ecosystems?

EMBRACING DISRUPTIVE INNOVATION

Much of my work as a business futurist and keynote speaker is on disruptive innovation; how to anticipate it, and how to capitalize on it. Disruptive innovation normally involves new technologies. The personal computer disrupted the electronic typewriter market. The digital camera disrupted the analog film-based camera market. The iPhone disrupted the mobile phone industry. SpaceX's reusable rockets are disrupting the space launch business. These are all new technologies.

There are two types of innovation: incremental innovation and disruptive innovation. Incremental innovation speaks for itself. Products and services are improved, incrementally, year after year. The 2020 Ford F150 pickup truck is a bit better than the 2019 model.

Incremental innovation is extremely powerful. We are optimizing our planet with incremental innovation, industry by industry, and country by country, but it's not the same thing as disruptive innovation. Disruptive innovation invalidates existing business models.

Disruptive innovation introduces a whole new way of doing things, usually delivering better outcomes for fewer dollars. Most recent examples involve technology. Uber and Airbnb are the over-used examples of our day. Both provided better user experiences at lower cost, and both have had enormous impact on their respective industries.

As mentioned many times in this book already, technology evolves along an exponential curve. And since most disruptive innovation is technology-driven, business executives are frequently caught off guard. The innovation seems insignificant in the early days, but the progress accelerates beyond comprehension, and you end up shellacked in the end.

One core difference between incremental and disruptive innovation is that incremental innovation comes from the center of expertise while disruptive innovation comes from the edges.

Incremental innovation comes from experts, specialists, and scientists who know the technology inside and out. Users make requests for product improvements, and the specialists tackle one suggestion after another. Suggestions also come from internal brainstorming, but the innovations are always improvements within existing usage patterns.

Institutional Blindness

"Institutional blindness" refers to the inability of people to see peripheral possibilities because they're too focused on their primary goals. If you're focused on improving an existing business model, it's difficult or even impossible to see alternative business models, even when they might be better than the existing version.

Daniel J. Simons and Christopher Chabris created a world-famous study in 1999 highlighting the impact of "selective attention" on perception and comprehension. In the study, they had three students wearing black t-shirts and three students wearing white t-shirts. Each team had one basketball and observers were asked to count how many completed passes the white t-shirted students made during a one-minute time period.

The video of this experiment is available on YouTube, and I first watched it myself in 2010. I followed the instructions and focused on the three students wearing white t-shirts, counting their throws as they mingled through and between the other students. After the minute had passed, the instructor asked if we had seen the gorilla. I thought it was a joke. I had no idea what he was talking about.

Turns out, during the one-minute period where I had been intently observing the students' activity, a man wearing a gorilla costume sauntered from the right side of the room to the middle of the group of students, did a little dance for the camera, and then walked out the left side of the room.

I never even noticed him. I was so stunned that I watched the entire video again. Yup, it was true. The gorilla had been there all along, but I literally didn't see him. I was flabbergasted.

This experiment is the best example I have ever found of selective attention and/or institutional blindness. When we're focused on particular problems, milestones, objectives, or outcomes, we become blind to everything else. Something can literally be right in front of our face, and we can miss it completely.

This hearkens back to the discussion of our conscious awareness, which I described in my TEDx Talk (and discussed in the Automation section). We only see what we're focused on. We miss 99.9996% of our own observations, because we're only consciously aware of roughly 40 things at one time. Institutional blindness refers to the 99.9996% of observations that we miss. Selective attention refers to the 0.0004% that we notice.

Incremental innovation is an amazingly powerful force, but it falls victim to selective attention. Experts, specialists, and scientists are very smart people, but they often miss seemingly obvious factors that are outside of their focus.

Sources of Disruptive Innovation

Disruptive innovation usually comes from that unobserved periphery. Imagine three industries that are different from each other, but related in some ways. There might be small overlaps between them. Disruptive innovation generally comes from those overlaps—i.e., areas that are on the periphery of each individual industry.

Peter Diamandis, founder of the X Prize Foundation, refers to these related industries as adjacent markets.

Apple disrupted the music business with their iTunes media library. That was an adjacent market. Apple wasn't in the music business, but its industry was related to the music business through the iPod MP3 player. Apple also disrupted the phone business with its iPhone, as did Google with the Android operating system. Those were adjacent markets.

The easiest way to identify adjacent markets is to write down a list of your largest suppliers, and then ask, "Who else do they sell to?" Those are adjacent markets. Next, write down a list of your largest customers, and then ask, "Who else do they buy from?" Those are adjacent markets. Within 30 minutes, you and your executive team can probably identify at least 20 or 30 adjacent markets.

Add your largest suppliers' and customers' industries to the list. Then, go down the list and ask in each case, "What are they doing poorly?" In many cases, they might be doing everything well. No problems. Many industries are operating well already, but there are invariably three or four that are quickly highlighted as poor performers.

They might be poorly run, have low-quality products, or have clumsy online user interfaces. Who knows? It could be anything. The bottom line is that these poor performers are ripe for disruption.

- Can you bring their business model in-house?
- Can you develop a better version of their business and steal their revenue?

These are new revenue opportunities. They are opportunities to disrupt someone else's business model. They represent an offensive business strategy.

Most businesses undervalue their operating relationships, including their suppliers, customers, and channel partners. All of those relationships are incredibly valuable. Together, they represent a go-to-market pipeline.

- What else can you sell through that same pipeline?

Technology is evolving so quickly that business executives instinctively take a defensive posture. They don't want someone to come along and "eat their lunch." Their primary focus is to protect their existing revenue streams.

That's the wrong focus! Business executives shouldn't be playing defense, not in today's chaotic business world. They need to be playing offense! They need to focus on who *else's* lunch they can eat. Stay on offense! Many companies will falter over the coming years. Focus on their weaknesses and look for new revenue opportunities. Be relentless, and seize any opportunities that leverage your strengths.

LinkedIn disrupted the recruiting industry. Amazon disrupted the book business with their Kindle e-reader. Uber Eats is disrupting the food delivery business, and Amazon is doing the same to the grocery business. Tesla, Google, and Apple are disrupting the automobile business. These are all adjacent markets.

On May 23, 2019, SpaceX launched a Falcon 9 rocket with 60 Starlink satellites on board. Those satellites will eventually become part of a 12,000+ satellite constellation in lower earth orbit, delivering high-speed internet connectivity to the entire globe. That's an adjacent market.

The origins of disruptive innovation are often mocked and ridiculed before they gain traction. Burt Rutan, a retired American aerospace engineer and entrepreneur, once said, "The day before something is a breakthrough, it's a crazy idea."

Where's the cutting edge of nutritional supplements? Where's the bleeding edge? Surprisingly often, it's in horseracing. It makes sense, because it's a less regulated industry, and owners have millions invested in their horses, but most aren't quite good enough to win. They'll try anything to see if it works.

That's where creatine came from. Creatine is a health supplement that helps muscles produce energy during heavy lifting or high-intensity exercise. I take creatine myself, as do many weightlifters and athletes. Before gaining traction in human markets, it was used in horseracing.

The benefits of vitamin D3 were proven effective in horseracing. The impact of zinc-loading on testosterone levels was observed in horseracing before going mainstream for human consumption. I'm sure research took place in other areas as well, but early applications included these adjacent markets.

Where's the cutting edge of online marketing? It's in porn and online gambling. That's where they test the latest lead magnets, wire frames, and conversion funnels. Because of the fierce competition in those fields, developers need to stay on the cutting edge, and they're willing to test all the latest tactics to improve conversion.

Jeff Walker is known for creating the Product Launch Formula. He also wrote the book "Launch" (2014, Morgan James Publishing). Jeff created an online conversion strategy that engaged prospects with high-quality free content, led them through a four-stage campaign, accumulated "social proof" along the way, and then asked for the sale during a limited-time 'launch' at the very end. It was hugely successful and has since been used by thousands of online information marketers.

The information marketing industry is definitely on the fringe of traditional e-commerce, but the success of the Product Launch Formula quickly got the attention of major companies including Apple. They "launch" all of their new products too, and they follow a similar sequence. There's a build-up as you get closer, leaks consistently slip out along the way, and anticipation increases until the product is finally released.

The Product Launch Formula is a disruptive innovation. It's a new way of engaging prospects, establishing trust, and building anticipation, all designed to increase sales conversions. It started in the fringe online information marketing industry, and then its success drove a migration to mainstream markets. That is almost always how it goes.

Ask yourself, "What's the fringe of my industry?" Find the crazy people in your field, and see what they're doing. Get on their email lists, and keep track of the solutions they're offering. Their efforts are leading indicators for disruptive innovation in the broader marketplace.

Here's another gem: Disruptive innovation often caters to the least profitable market segment first. This is described beautifully in "The Innovator's Dilemma" (2016, Harvard Business Review Press) by Clayton M. Christensen.

- Who is your least profitable market segment?

These are generally the customers you hate. Sometimes, it would be easier if they just disappeared. They have no money, they're always complaining, and they're a pain in the neck. Disruptive innovation often caters to them first.

What do all businesses do? Do they cater to those irritating customers? No! Instead, they cater to the *most* profitable market segment. Every company in every industry automatically focuses on their premium products and services, which are sold to their premium customers. Why? Because that's where the money is!

Why do bank robbers rob banks? Because that's where the money is!

This is a natural and logical incentive structure. Salespeople make the most money by selling the premium products. Companies earn the highest gross profit from the most expensive products. It makes perfect sense to disproportionately put your efforts there, but who gets left behind? The least profitable market segment.

Take some time to brainstorm this reality. Identify your least profitable market segment and ask yourself what they want. More often than not, they want a simpler and less expensive solution. It's the same in almost every industry.

We've discussed two models for anticipating disruptive innovation:

1. Disruptive innovation comes from adjacent markets.

2. Disruptive innovation caters to the least profitable market segment first.

This simple process can help you identify the customers demanding new solutions, the nature of their demands, and the place from which new solutions might come.

Strategic Framework

I facilitate strategy sessions with executive teams using this framework, and it always amazes me how quickly new revenue opportunities are identified, and how accurately disruptive innovations are anticipated. It's simply a question of breaking institutional blindness and honing attention by using structured questions. I always teach them one last model to tie it all together: look up, look down, look side-to-side.

Look up. Those are your premium products. That's where your gross profit comes from. You need that gross profit! Innovation boils down to just one concept, and it can be summarized in just two words: budgeting failure.

True innovation requires that you try new things, and that implies that your experiments might not work. You need a budget for those experiments. Innovation = budgeting failure.

Jeff Bezos, founder of Amazon, once said, "If you know it's gonna work, it's *not* an experiment!" Innovation requires trying new things, and that costs money. So continue to focus on your premium products. You need that money to be innovative.

Look down. This is where disruptive innovation comes from. It caters to the least profitable market segment first. Think about those customers, and update your evaluations on a regular basis. Look for companies providing simpler and less expensive solutions. Monitor the success or failure of those solutions, and consider adopting similar innovations if you notice solutions gaining traction in the marketplace.

Look side-to-side. These are your new revenue opportunities. These are your adjacent markets. Maintain your list of adjacent markets, and monitor opportunities for expansion within those fields. Stay on offense! Who else's lunch can *you* eat?!

The best way to thank an author is to post a review on Amazon. If you enjoyed this book, please take a moment to post a review online. Thank you.

THINK BIGGER

The message of this book is to think bigger. Think bigger about what's possible. This is a time of extraordinary change. The whole world is upside down, but that spells opportunity for entrepreneurs and business leaders. As I said at the beginning, we have never needed your leadership more than we do today.

I study visionary business leaders including Steve Jobs, Bill Gates, Elon Musk, and Jeff Bezos, and they have lots of similarities. For starters, they think about possibilities, not limitations. They're not concerned with obstacles. They're focused on opportunities. Second, they adopt incredibly ambitious goals. They are visionary leaders, and their approach has predictable consequences.

First, they inspire everyone around them. People want to be part of the excitement. They want to be where the action is. And when you think bigger, people are naturally attracted to your vision. Your employees are inspired when you're shooting for bigger goals. Your customers are inspired as well. Even your competitors are inspired when you're thinking bigger!

People want to make a difference. They want to change the world. It's a natural human instinct, especially when they're young. Momentum trumps everything. People want to be where the action is. Thinking bigger automatically pulls people in. The best way to engage people (such as your employees and your customers) is to take a stand for what you believe in, and do something big.

Secondly, when you're thinking bigger, quite often, you have almost no competition along the way, because most people don't have the courage to truly innovate and try new things. If you're trying something new, by definition, you're on your own. Success is more likely if you're not competing against someone else, and the easiest way to be in that situation is to try something new.

Many business leaders are known for this type of thinking. Richard Branson is a great example. He also has dozens of great quotes. I love quotes. I literally buy books of quotes. Here's my favorite Richard Branson quote: "The fastest way to become a *millionaire* is to start out as a *billionaire*, and then start an airline!" Brilliant.

Richard Branson started Virgin Galactic. You can't get much bigger than that! Does he have any competition? Not much. There are a few companies trying to do similar things, but he's mostly flying solo.

What about Elon Musk? He's like a personal hero to me. I love the way he thinks. He thinks in first principles, meaning he boils things down to the most fundamental truths and then reasons up from there. It's a fascinating alternative to the analogy-based thinking patterns most others use.

Elon Musk founded SpaceX, the first private corporation to deliver cargo to the International Space Station (ISS). No private company had ever done that before, and they're reusing their rockets. They're sending the rocket up and then bringing the first (and largest) stage back down, landing it on a barge out in the Atlantic Ocean or on a platform adjacent to the launch pad.

More recently, they've begun recovering the upper stage fairings as well. Those fairings cost about six million dollars to fabricate. Musk once said, "Guys, imagine we had six million dollars on a pallet of cash. Six million dollars is falling through the sky. Wouldn't we try to catch it?" SpaceX engineers tried many different approaches, and the result is almost complete reusability of their rockets.

This is a perfect example of thinking in first principles. The cost of sending a rocket to the ISS is about $60 million. The exact amount depends on the cargo, but it's roughly $60 million. What does the fuel cost? Someone asked me this four years ago. I guessed $10 million. That seemed reasonable to me.

Not even close. The right answer is just $200,000! That's about one-300th of the total cost. So if you can reuse the hardware (the rockets themselves), you bring down the cost function by 100 fold or more. Now, that's disruptive innovation!

No other launch company has mastered rocket reusability like SpaceX. Others are working on it, including Jeff Bezo's Blue Origin, but they have a tiny fraction of SpaceX's experience. SpaceX successfully landed their 50th rocket booster in March 2020.

This also creates an incredible cost advantage of their Starlink satellite network. They have the cheapest launch costs in the world, so they're able to launch their satellites more cheaply than anyone else. Bold leadership in one area often parlays into bold leadership in another.

Elon Musk saw the inefficiencies in the rocket launch industry right from the start. He knew that reusable rockets were essential to bring the cost structure down, so he and his team developed the means to land the first stage back on Earth.

The first time they pulled it off was on December 21, 2015, and their employees partied like it was 1999. The average age of SpaceX employees is 27. That makes them millennials. Millennials get a bad rap. People accuse them of being lazy, apathetic, and entitled. It's not true. Millennials will work harder than anyone you've ever hired if you give them something inspiring to work towards.

Millennials are just young, that's all. Actually, they're not even that young anymore. Anyone born after 1980 is a millennial, and the generation born after 2000 is Gen Z. The point is that young people want to do cool things. They want to change the world. Baby boomers and Gen X (including myself) had similar aspirations when we were young.

People get excited when you think bigger. It's not just a cliché. It actually works that way. When you're doing something big, your employees (including millennials) get fired up and engaged in the process. Obviously, we don't all have the luxury of building rockets designed to fly to Mars, but we all have the option to think bigger about the projects we're tackling.

Earlier in this book, I mentioned that we're literally optimizing the planet with incremental innovations. It's true. Every industry is contributing to that trend. The world is getting better, and your business is part of that too. You're improving your systems every year. The problem is that most employees are never told about these larger realities.

As a business leader, it's your responsibility to speak with your people about these broader trends. We're optimizing the planet. It's exciting. Tell your people. It's a big deal. Tell them how your investments in innovation are contributing to this global optimization process.

Elon Musk also founded Tesla. Any competition there? Well, yes, actually, there is, but nobody's buying those other brands. Tesla still sells more electric vehicles than all of the other brands combined. Why? Because Tesla is standing defiantly by their mission, building *only* electric vehicles, and people are inspired by their vision.

Tesla released their Model 3 in 2016 and racked up more than 500,000 reservations, more than any car launch in history. People get excited about visionary goals. It's true. Thinking bigger inspires everyone. Tesla and SpaceX are proving that every single day.

Tesla also introduced their Powerwall. It hangs on your wall, attaches to the solar panels on your roof, allowing it to charge during the day, so you can use the power at night, and disconnect from the power grid entirely. These are the battery packs that many Hawaiian homeowners purchased to sidestep the electric utility. Any competition? Nope. None.

Tesla is still building their first Gigafactory in Nevada. Once complete, it will be the largest building in the world by footprint. That one Gigafactory will more than double the global production capacity of lithium ion batteries, and that doesn't even include their second Gigafactory in New York, their third in China, or their fourth in Germany, all under construction. Any competition? Nothing even close.

There's a magic to thinking bigger, and the COVID-19 pandemic has blown all the traditional limitations out the window. Everything is on the table. Anything is possible. Embrace this moment. Reimagine tomorrow's economy. As difficult as this time is for many, it's also the opportunity of a lifetime!

ADDITIONAL RESOURCES

Patrick Schwerdtfeger has created an online training program for those who wish to learn more about his strategies. It's called the "Scale Academy" and encourages business owners and executive decision-makers to think bigger about their business and scale operations to a higher level.

Book Reviews

Please review this book on Amazon. Whether you think it deserves five stars, one star, or something in between, reviews are extremely important. We hope you have found value in the book and hope you'll share your thoughts for future readers to see.

Bulk Book Orders

Discounts are available for bulk book orders. Contact us if you're interested in purchasing this book for your team. Available formats include both paperback and hardcover, and custom messages can be included with larger quantities.

Media Interviews

Are you a journalist, TV show host, YouTuber, podcaster, or blogger? Patrick Schwerdtfeger is available for media interviews and special events. Contact us to discuss your target audience and content objectives.

Keynote Speaking

Patrick Schwerdtfeger speaks at dozens of corporate events each year. His primary topics include (1) Disruptive Innovation, (2) Artificial Intelligence, and (3) Blockchain. Contact us to check availability and pricing.

Innovation Training

Do you need to cultivate a culture of innovation within your team? We facilitate online and offline training to harness innovative potential within your organization, both now and reliably into the future. Contact us for details.

Contact Information

The easiest way to contact the author is by email or through his website.

https://www.patrickschwerdtfeger.com
Email: patrick@bookpatrick.com

Made in the USA
Coppell, TX
07 October 2020